KANDAN, THE PATRIOT

K. S. VENKATARAMANI

GYAN

Published by

GYAN

Gyan Publishing House
5, Ansari Road
Daryaganj, New Delhi-110002
Phone: 011-47034999, 9811692060
E-mail: books@gyanbooks.com

Distribution Network
gyanbooks.com
India, USA, Canada, UK, Australia

ISBN: 978-93-7316-225-6 (PB)

First Published, 1932

2nd Impression 2025

Printed at: Gyan Press, Delhi.

KANDAN, THE PATRIOT
Author: K. S. VENKATARAMANI

KANDAN, THE PATRIOT

KANDAN THE PATRIOT

KANDAN THE PATRIOT

BY

K. S. VENKATARAMANI

TO

THE UNKNOWN VOLUNTEER

IN INDIA'S FIGHT FOR FREEDOM

CONTENTS

CHAPTER I

THE TODDY-SHOP AT AKKUR

(1)

AKKUR is a beauty spot on the short branch line from Mayavaram to Tranquebar, the Queen of the Coromandel coast.

There was a stillness in the evening air, though the sea lay to the east barely three miles off. The breeze had not yet set in. It seemed to loiter round the trembling crest of the waves, kissing the water-line and scattering the foam that embroidered the endless shores of the sea.

It was five minutes past four. No. 9 had just left for Mayavaram. The small, vagabondish train of five coaches was pulled by an old battered engine that had seen better days on the main line when it ran as the Tuticorin Express. Still it had a bit of its old vigour which it showed by plenty of rattling noise. It loved its work on the new branch line though the virgin track seemed to groan under the vicious strokes of this old, battered engine. It sped and lilted, lilted and sped, and thundered along the shining rails with a rollicking joy in motion.

(2)

The whistle that sped No. 9 on its lonely track was the signal for the rally of life at the toddy-shop at Akkur. This pleasure shop for the poor stood like a hermitage in a cocoanut garden facing a wide sheet of water, the village tank, to which the workmen came for their bath every evening after the day's hard work in the fields. The bath at the matin hour cooled their heated bodies, and this pleasant toddy drink made up for the loss of warmth.

The toddy-shop at Akkur was the eldest born of the railroad from Mayavaram to Tranquebar. The construction of this branch line had rushed in such a flood of money that the toddy-shop, from its opening day, hummed like a bee-hive, and the silver of the sweated poor flowed into it in an unbroken stream.

The moment it was known that the branch line was sanctioned, the leading excise contractor of the place, one who had become a millionaire on this cheap drink for the poor, had sent in his garland of roses knitted on threads of gold, and a basket of lemons, ripe and yellow, to the local official gods who anoint and consecrate a new toddy-shop. The net result was that, before the first sod was cut on the Mayavaram-Tranquebar line, the toddy-shop at Akkur was in full working order.

Chockalinga, the local magnate, eventually became the lessee, as it was deftly suggested to him that the lord of thirty thousand cocoanut trees was the proper lessee of a toddy-shop nearby—gold in one's own land, should it be worked by another?

Chockalinga was young and unmarried, imaginative and enterprising. His apprentice hand was always prompted by a curious and experimenting mind, with deadly effect on ancestral riches. He had already exhausted several forms of pioneering enterprise for the industrial regeneration of his country: rice mill, bus service and rail-road contract. The Tamil genius readily lends itself to three kinds of venture: rice-mill, bus service, and toddy-shop, not to speak of the primary enterprise of cooking and catering.

Why not try a toddy-shop though it was generally considered by the idle folk as dishonourable? If rearing cocoanut trees is a merit, why should tapping them for this sweet and mild drink of the Tamils be a sin? Part at least of the wages he paid generously to his idle tenants would come back to him. Thus he argued just to ease his own conscience and reveal to himself the incisive quality of his mind.

Chockalinga Mudaliar of course, could not attend to the details of this promising business. So he left practically its real administration into the hands of his friend, the leading excise contractor of the place. And he saw to it, with such cheap and plentiful supply of toddy and his own experience in organising the drink trade, that the shop hummed like a bee-hive.

(3)

The rally to a toddy-shop at the evening hour is a sight indeed! And at Akkur the toddy-shop was new and the rally of the men was really a delighted run from the fields with the joy of a child that goes to the sweet-meat shop straight from the school. Toddy was a new drink to almost everyone round about Akkur except for a few aged veterans to whom distance had never been a bar.

It was a miscellaneous group that had gathered itself there that evening. But it was divided into well-knit clans for the call of pleasure.

Nandan, Mookkan, and Katteri led the band of aged veterans who rather seemed to think that this choice drink of the stalwarts had been cheaply brought within the lazy reach of all.

Irullan, Karuppan, and Irullappan led the band of daring youngsters who were as quick and good at work as at revolt. They walked into the toddy-shop with the swagger of youth.

And Nochi, the *talayari*, stood all by himself, firm and motionless like a sculptured god in granite, in the infinite beauty of his bare brawn and muscle.

These two groups belonged to the 'untouchable' classes. But they were the most intimate in touch with Mother Earth. They were the real tillers of the soil.

Govindan, Pavadai, and Nallan marched with their own kinsmen and friends with greater decorum and more of suppressed joy but with a prick of conscience shining guiltily over their lowered faces. For they came from the proud *podayachi* clan, which once formed the backbone of the Tamil infantry in the valorous days of the Chola and Nayak kings of Tanjore. Still they showed a spark of their old fire in starting the angry and incessant quarrels of the toddy-shop. They took the offensive in all matters and broke the massive strength of Nandan, Mookkan, and Katteri: Irullan, Karuppan, and Irullappan.

This straggling army of workers had not a square inch of ground in all the wide spaces on earth either for home or for field, but toiled on with sweat on brow in the narrow ruts of an ancient system now ploughed to deep mire by modern economic forces. Though accepted neither on earth nor in Heaven, they showed the gaiety of princes in the toddy-shop.

(4)

Nandan, the leader of the first group, who never got himself reconciled to these new votaries to drink, began his usual lament to his friend.

"Mookka, look at these fellows, how crude and vulgar they are: one is born to drink and never madè; they can't learn the graces in a day, the sober and the gentle way. These youngsters don't know even to raise the pot gracefully to the lips and sip the nectar with a gentle whir. They drink it gulping it down as if it were a decoction for fever. Pooh! look at our *talayari*. Nochi may be a fine fellow in the field with his long pole and lashing whip in hand. But he's nowhere here in the toddy-shop, like a fish on land."

"Or like a policeman among thieves." Katteri tried to improve the figure of speech.

Nandan was seventy years old but had a firm grip of the pot. He spoke slowly and in a grave voice, and in his roiling looks there was the bright twinkle of experience. He showed at every turn a slight resentment and contempt at the so many raw newcomers to a very ancient pleasure, who had incidentally sent up the price of toddy and sent down its quality.

"Nanda, we must teach them a lesson one day with the rod, so that they may know we are masters at least here. Nochi may be our *talayari*, but here in the toddy-shop he's no better than a broken pot. We must teach him his place here," Mookkan hissed in a low tone.

Katteri, who was till now preoccupied with the third pot, turned round his fierce looks and growled with a vacant laugh, "Mookka, you are as foolish as ever, and don't know, for all your age and bulk, the true cause of things."

Mookkan coughed and spat dissent, but heeding it not Katteri proceeded, "Nochi rules only over our little clan of pariahs but the secret of his power is that he is backed by Nallan who is in turn backed by our lord. Look at it deeply, Nanda, you understand these matters better than our cousin Mookkan, for all his burly head, eagle nose, and big body—we toil all day long and barely earn the surplus money for this trifling and only joy of our lives—a pot a day."

Katteri rolled his eyes in anger and began in a voice of thunder: "A pot of toddy is the only friend the pariah has the world over. Have we milk or honey, fruits or flowers, or any of the dainties that go to feed our ruling folk? Have we an inch of ground for home or field? Even our wedded wives are but our master's farm servants; our darling child is the shepherd-boy of the *pannai* roaming over mud and mire, stones and thorns, tending the cows whose milk goes only to feed another. Nanda, tell me,—you have shrewd eyes, what is a pariah's life worth but for a pot of toddy?"

Both Nandan and Mookkan violently nodded their heads in approval of this declamation, and Katteri continued taking encouragement from their nods and another pot of toddy. "Nallan makes five times the money we make for all our sweated labour. Do you think it's all made the right way? Nallan is in charge of the granary, and you know that Mr. Mudaliar is away twenty days out of thirty. There is a rat-hole in the granary and Nallan is in special charge of it day and night."

Katteri growled at this good luck of another man. For he had in his younger days the best reputation as a granary-rat, and the long hands which Nature had given him in its most sympathetic mood he had made the finest use of.

Nandan, Mookkan, and Katteri had to face none of the keener problems of life that ordinarily fall to the lot of these semi-serfs. For, Chockalinga's father had given them, in recognition of some signal service done to him in an hour of peril, a monthly pension of two *kalams* of paddy. The signal act of service was that they had raided a hostile village in the neighbourhood and harvested the fields, all at dead of night, and carried off the booty before dawn. And this freedom and leisure they used for cultivating the fine art of conversation, like seemingly prosperous lawyers at the club table.

(5)

The other group was equally busy with the tongue and the pot: Irullan, Karuppan, and Irullappan.

"Irulla, how did you find the money for the day? I've been put to very hard straits. You've had no coolie work in the fields for a week," asked Karuppan who was in the regular service of Mr. Mudaliar as a *pannaial*.

Irullan too was once in the regular service but fared ill in all team work. Though he worked the hardest of all, he found that the blame for the arrears of work was always thrown on his head. Finally he was dismissed as he incurred the anger of Nochi in the division of the spoils of a theft in which Irullan did all the daring and Nochi had all the sharing.

"Well, Karuppa, how to find the money! I beat my wife till I got it."

"How?"

"How? This way," he brandished his brawny right hand stroking the air and said, "till she gave up her secret treasure—the little silver anklet."

"The silver anklet of your dear boy, now no more!"

"Yes, she treasured it that she might weep hours over it and do no work. I'll have no more of it, and the bother is over. But tell me, how did you manage for the day, Karuppa? Your wages too are in arrears for over a fortnight and your lord is always away speeding in and out in his motor car on some election round or other."

"Yes, Irulla, it's better to starve and die than to work in this wretched *pannai* where cattle are better housed and cared for than men. This place is good only for thieves and cheats like Nochi and Nallan. I hadn't a wink of sleep overnight. You know the big *karuvelam* tree by the channel, uprooted by the recent floods, and so many coveting it. With borrowed axe I worked at it the whole of last night, and made five bundles of firewood. I walked the ten miles to Mayavaram at dead of night with my wife and my boy carrying the heavy loads, two each, over secret ways and thorny paths, often knee deep in hidden holes and sunken mire—well, only to sell them just at break of dawn for half their fair price ; stolen things, you know, even trees whose bowels have been ripped open, carry a stolen look everywhere even miles away ; sold the five bundles for a rupee,—here's the silver piece intact."

Karuppan chuckled with joy and Irullan cast measured glances of envy at the rupee, round and full, gleaming with the glory of King George's imprint which meant to thirsty Karuppan five gallons of toddy.

Karuppan continued the story, the silver disc attracting the full eye of the house, " I've the whole rupee now, here it's—my wife begged of me an anna for glass bangles—and what do you think I did ? I twisted her hands till she cried no more for bangles and I followed it up with a conclusive slap on her face. My boy who bore the bundles bravely through mire and thorn, asked for an anna for two *iddlies*—I gave him a blow on the mouth and a kick on the knees. Here is the full rupee saved from foul attack, and Irulla, is this not good for three days, on the most liberal scale?"

"But, Karuppa, if you are caught and whipped for the theft! There's Nochi, the *talayari*, and Nallan too."

"I'm not afraid of them. The drink-shop is a common place for all. What if he is the *talayari*? I'll buy him over with a pot. Well, Nochi *anne*, what news and how is your luck for the day?"

"Well, lazy loons, mind your own business. Karuppa, where did you steal that rupee?"

"Dear cousin, if I've stolen it, you have your share in it."

"Then you are welcome as it makes a different matter for both of us."

"Nochi, you are indeed a fine fellow and deserve to be our *talayari* for ever. Long live the granary-heaps and the rat-holes and our dear Nochi," cried in one voice Irullan, Karuppan, and Irullappan drinking to his health.

Irullappan was glad that in the increasing tumult of intoxication no questions were put to him to disclose his resources for the day. For, he had quite a month ago replenished his exchequer by the theft of a gold necklace of a guest in the very garden house of Mr. Mudaliar and had the prudence and economy to negotiate the sale of the stolen property with the salesman of the toddy-shop and get the proceeds allotted for a month's drink. And he pretended to drink on credit.

(6)

The third group, Govindan, Pavadai, and Nallan, were the men of quality at the toddy-shop. They were equally busy with the tongue and the pot. Nallan was their acknowledged leader and held the position of *maniyam* or chief executive field-officer of Mudaliar's *pannai*.

"Nalla, you are growing discontented of late with Mr. Mudaliar's ways. Why not we give up this job of 'rat-holes' and minor thefts, and do some honest work elsewhere in some humbler place, work that would please both God and man." Govindan, his cousin, gently prodded Nallan. Govindan never missed a chance to promote some misunderstanding between his cousin and Mr. Mudaliar. "We starve day and night while our lord feasts in his house strange men from far-away places, like a prince royal, gay and reckless. The times have changed and the old-time prestige has gone for ever from Akkur *pannai* land and name. And as Kandan, our reforming saint, says, there will soon be a terrible crash everywhere."

"Yes, Govinda, you are right. My pay is due for over eighteen months. The chief agents have their own way, and the master is always away. Half the land lies fallow for the year, and the *pannai* is discontented for all my scowls and Nochi's whips; and Mr. Mudaliar is head over ears lost in the Council elections, just only to beat the other dark fellow from Negapatam. Our wages go to the feeding and fattening of idle official folk."

"You talk quite like Kandan and you've caught his accent well indeed, Nalla. The harvest we raise with so much of hard work we've no share in it, as you say. Why should we put up with this state of affairs? Dear cousin, lead us bravely on and we would follow you to death. Nochi will bring his men to your side and help you with the bravest and cleverest of the lot. Dare he go against your wish? Gather all these idle fellows by you, these knaves and thieves together, and make men of them, as Kandan says. Well, do some clean, good work; you alone can show us the way. I swear by this sacred drink that I'll stand by you to death."

"Yes, that is just what Kandan says so fervently and in noble speech. It flatters us: Stand together and work for the common good and give up this drink—a curse indeed."

"Yes, dear brother, let us obey his words as words from Heaven." Pavadai spoke with feeling. "Kandan is a saint, a noble soul. I saw him in his *ashrama* this morning, distributing *charka* and *khaddar* to the suffering poor. People say he is mighty rich in Natal and as great as the Collector *dorai* at Tanjore, if only he cared to be that. He was kind and good to me." Pavadai was the younger brother of Nallan and a bright lad of sixteen.

"Pavadai, Kandan is kind to all, and has a special liking for you. For you alone of us here have had a little schooling. It's a pity I was not put to school; and a double pity that I was not able to put you up for higher study. I'd even have made the rat-holes deeper in the grain-heaps, but this toddy-shop came in the way, alas! And it has thrown us all on the mound of waste—but everything is going wrong. Mr. Mudaliar too cannot carry on like this for long."

"Though young, brother, I too feel that there must come a grand change in our lives and that this toddy-shop must go. It has been the unmaking of our family. Kandan is the man to make men of us. Let us follow his words. Maybe, he could even change Mr. Mudaliar too some day,—there's a magnet glow in his eyes, a purifying fire in his speech."

"Change our Mudaliar! as well you can wash an ass into a horse: that's impossible, Pavadai, even if the gods came straight from Heaven. The young flesh is already too deep in the mire. You should see his aged mother with her weeping eyes, weeping at the truant ways of her unmarried boy. It breaks her heart to—there comes Kandan,—yes, with the pure glow of kindness in his face as you say. Let us all prostrate ourselves before him. Though we don't follow his words let us honour him."

Nallan spoke with the ring of sincerity in his voice. There was the tender hush of expectancy everywhere in the toddy-shop as in a fruit garden just before the burst of rains in the season.

CHAPTER II

DEW-DROPS ON LOTUS-BUDS

(1)

A MAGNIFICENT bridge, far superior to the traffic it carries, and far surpassing the paltry traditions of the D. P. W. (Department of Public Works), spans the river Adyar very near its mouth. The river is broad, but carries no flood to the sea except during moonsoon hours. And the sea has de-sexed the river. For under the swell of tidal action there is a perpetual flow under the bridge of clear, blue, sparkling sea-water. Standing in the middle of the arching bridge and leaning lightly on the massive parapet wall, you gain such a view of land and sea, and the glory of the sun, rising or setting, that it makes a lasting impression on you.

This fine bridge leads you with a graceful curve to the east to the gardens of the Theosophical Society, solemn and still with an air of experiments and absorbed enquiry into the first problems of life. Everything is fresh and green, sweet and fragrant.

Even the breeze that roams from sea to land seems to feel the loitering calm of the place.

The guest-house edging on the banks of the Adyar and by the side of the famous banyan tree, is indeed a thing of beauty. Man and Nature have both striven in comradeship to make the spot idyllic. The eternal murmur of the sea comes home as the lisping cries of a child that calls for its mother. Adyar echoes to the murmur of the sea in rolling eddies that go winding up the river.

Little birds sing the music in the air, numerous little birds that fly nameless in a tropical country. Oblivious of the sweated dust of the roads and the hard work of the stone-breaker and the road-mender, a stray pleasure-canoe of a white man, proud and trim, goes up and down the river, with its little sails of pure white shining over the blue water like a summer cloud in the sky. There is a touch of alien triumph in the victorious glide of the decked wood on water.

(2)

It was the same evening and the same hour as at Akkur: five minutes past four which sent No. 9 puffing and rattling, sounding the whistle that was the roll-call and the speeding time for the toddy-shop at Akkur.

The guest-house at Adyar in the glory of the evening sun, stood like a virgin who had stepped out of her sylvan shade, the banyan tree, for a short walk.

Rajeswari Bai was pacing up and down the verandah of the guest house in a restless but charming mood. She seemed the very soul of the place, in the chaste beauty of her virgin looks. She had just arrived in the morning.

Rajeswari Bai was looking up and down the undulating road which crept on winding like the bed of a dry river till it lost itself in the green gloom of cocoanut trees. The traffic on the main road lay two furlongs off and a thin hum had settled on the top of the banyan tree. The hoot of every car came shrill, piercing the thin hum of traffic and sent a strange thrill through Rajeswari's queenly mind. From the top floor of the guest-house, the Adyar Bridge was a thing of spanned beauty and measured splendour. The massiveness mellowed into gracious looks of strength and liquid beauty from the just distance of the guest-house.

Stealing his steps like the cat that goes to the cheese or the spider that leaps on to the fly, Rangaswami came running along the foot-path by the side of the river, ran up the staircase, and from behind, gently patted Rajeswari on her shoulders, soft as new fallen snow on peaks. She was lost in a twilight dream of dances, and a reverie of half expectations. She just gave a start—another in her place would have screamed for help.

"For a palpitating heart, dear Ranga, this back-patting is no cure. But you are as romantic and foolish as ever; a year of critical change for all has wrought no change in you." Rajeswari chided him in a mingled voice of love and anger.

"Dear Rajee, I was only planning a pleasant surprise in an original way if possible."

"Your experienced head clerk, I suppose, was asked to draft the plan with a note?"

"Dear Rajee, don't be squeamish after a year's long separation—just for the pleasure of cracking jokes, hurting the tender thoughts of love. Remember your words when we last parted at the Victoria Terminus—words that gave me joy for a year and kept me up in the wretched official world that has become my lot, alas!"

"What, already discontented—with five hundred a month, and pomp and power! Why, you remember your own statistics in London, which you used so well at every meeting; the average earning power of an Indian a penny a day."

"Well, I know better now. I then talked from figures; now I can talk from life; that our masses are the poorest and the most ignorant of such lots in the world. But I fear the remedies are in their own hands. Government can do but little."

"How well you have caught the official slang in a year!"

"Rajee, I came here to talk of finer things than the official slang, or the lot of the poor!"

"But is there anything finer?"

"Yes, Rajee is."

She blushed a little but it was more the flush of anger that reddened her face than thoughts of love.

"In every way, what is life to me, worth even with two thousands a day, without you, Rajee. You must decide now. All the problems that racked our brains at Oxford for three years and more for our country's weal, we could best solve together now in a practical way. Work is everything. Talk, schemes, and wise words are of no use now; we have done it all enough these wasted years, and the country's call is for deeds, direct action at the very base of life, the village."

"Yes, quite so, but I view the mode of work, Ranga, in another way. Only, work outside the Government ranks will help the poor. Government have failed to be in touch with the pulse of the poor. If at all, just only to know how much more they can tap!"

"Nothing can and will be done effectively without the aid of Government in modern life, but frothy talk and foaming speeches. I've seen it all, though before I often thought like you, Rajee. It's impossible. Private effort will prove in vain like the dash of the raging sea against the ageless and smiling rocks. In any event, whatever we decide upon, let us decide it together when we begin our wedded life."

Rajeswari vigorously pouted her lips, and that made her the more beautiful.

"Rajee, you must decide now. A life gifted like yours is not meant to sail alone—the most beautiful ship ever built, why should it lie idle in the dock waiting for ever for an impossible cargo of diamonds?"

"Then you ask her to carry a cargo of coal?" Rajeswari shot an arrow.

It was a sharp thrust, for it contained a veiled allusion to Rangan's swarthy complexion. Rangan took such things always very pleasantly as a kind of penalty for his inordinate fondness for metaphors and similes that came tumbling down like pebbles in a mountain spate.

He ventured a belated reply, "Yes, yes, so that the whole world may not lack warmth and light."

Rangan had excellent powers of recuperation. Otherwise, how could a poor and homeless lad become an I. C. S., and an Assistant Collector, at the age of twenty-five.

Rangan paused a moment surveying the scene around him and said.

"Look yonder, Rajee, the banyan tree seems to wait, praying for a kiss of your feet with its wind-swept branches bowing low to the ground. Let us go to its inviting shade of green, and spell the joy of minutes, of fleeting seconds, and pour into each other's the cellared wine of a year's joy."

(3)

"Ranga, life is more serious than you and I thought of it while at Oxford. The call of the country has, for me at any rate, silenced the call of home and love, of leisured, rich, idle, contemplative and pretending life."

Rangan reared himself up a little, like a serpent, startled at the strange sincerity in her voice and the warm patriotic glow in her eyes. The Assistant Collector, who sent to prison in Guntur so many patriots a day, knew at least how to read the whole history of a life in a word and a look.

Rajeswari continued turning her neck loftily, "The world is in a ferment, though you see it not now with your official eye. We are breaking everything old that we may build something new on a higher valley of life. Our eyes glued to the text-books and the sports of boys saw it not at Oxford. It's clear to me even in these five minutes that your one year of office has ruined you and all the ideals of work for the poor that stirred your college career. It's a sin for an Indian to toil at the desk in these critical days when the making of a new India is going on before our very eyes under the glorious leadership of the greatest living man in the world. Shall our hands remain idle?"

"Dear Rajee, I've called you here by wire just to let you know what a great fight I'm making for my country from within. Fight the King from within—that is one way of doing things. I was prepared for the other and seemingly more patriotic work. But God has willed it for me in His own way. Courage, patriotic courage, if one has it deep down his heart, is never lost, by change of place or habits. Like complexion, Rajee, it is an inheritance with the flesh. It rolls in the blood. I shall tell you the inner story of my year's life as a civilian. You know that Guntur is in the thick of the fight. The poor fellows at the top seem to think that the great nationalistic movement could be put down with a few *lathi* charges and bullet shots. I wrote note after note, which swelled into essays, to the Member in charge. All through I carried on in my own way, though the police chiefs gave trouble. Yet from my talk with my chief this morning I gather things are brightening up, and soon there will be a change of policy and of heart, though as a penalty for my patriotic attitude I'm now transferred to the quieter Tanjore. That is the price I have paid. But it matters not for me. Dear Rajee, is this not also patriotic work? I challenge."

Rajeswari was silent for a few minutes as if in deep reflection.

"I did my work so well and independently that I am now under orders of transfer to Tanjore, a quieter place and my own district. I've still a week of joining time. That is why I telegraphed to you. In this hour, your presence is the best solace and guide to me. Pray, give me your final approval. I know you would put questions like this. I know you were taking a heroic part in the Bombay struggle. I know you are noted by the Government of India. Already telegraphic instructions have been received to watch your movements lest you disturb the quiet of this Province."

"Yes, Ranga, my love for you has taken me to the South. I have chosen to work here with you or against you, as it pleases God. Things are deeper than what you say they are. Your arguments are mere quibbles of a clever speaker. The true work of a patriot lies now outside the Government ranks. It might have been done through Government agencies some fifty years ago. Nobody did it then and now it is all too late even for the best men. The social order is crying and breaking for a change. No might on earth can stop it for an hour."

Rajeswari in the excess of emotion waved her hands in the air, which frightened two sparrows making love to each other on a lofty branch of the big banyan tree.

"The centre has shifted from there. Now we must work only from without. If you care to follow me through thick and thin and share with me in the real fight, and sacrifice your five hundred—I'm still yours, dear Ranga."

Taking a deep breath she continued: "Bombay has done, no doubt, some brave and wonderful things these three months and more. But it's all the first scene of the first act of a great five-act drama. I've come all the way a thousand miles, not to woo and wed and make merry, but to convert you to the larger cause of love of our Mother, the cause of our country. You will gain me and your country if you lose the I. C. S. Resign your job and join the Congress ranks, and work for the masses. If only you have seen the brimming tears of sorrow running down their pale cheeks! Brave imprisonment and *lathi* charges and carry the flag of our country to undreamt-of heights of honour—then this frail hand and body is yours for ever—so that the children sprung of our loins may see the light of day in a free country."

Quick of mind, Rangan saw the tidal wave of patriotism flooding the beautiful river winding higher and higher up. Rajee seemed but a fair flower dancing like foam on the lips of the whirling eddy that rolled along the swift current of the sea, higher and higher up the Adyar river.

" Dear Rajee, the only daughter of a millionaire and the darling of an ancient house, I would plead,—whence this strange anguish of a fanatic's soul? Pity for the poor whom no flood of tears can make clean, rich, or better but their own unremitting, proud self-help, effort and manly toil! Nature has meant your queenly beauty and royal looks for palace halls and not for prison cells. I know from my official knowledge of things what an awful fate and dire suffering awaits the patriot in this country, and it's no joke to cut the tentacles of this octopus of a British lion—I mean its manes."

Rangan breathed a minute of pause just to recover himself from the sunstroke of his own wild metaphors.

"Again, Rajee, you can't change a nation at one impetuous stroke of the pen in a day, as you and all the Congress people want to do. I'd argue like this, but I know it is of no avail with you in your present frame of mind: as well bid the sea not to rush up the Adyar river and fill its fair-fresh water banks with the bitter, salt sea-flood. The tide of nationalism is rising up, and women once caught in its swirl are no good arguing with."

But Rajeswari looked amazed at the tone of Rangan's speech. She couldn't help asking him: "But whence this profound change, Ranga? All your socialistic tenets that fascinated me your slave and co-worker on a hundred platforms in London, where are they now?—wiped off in the flood of a safe five hundred a month, and the pomp and power of office? You were once the most fervid of socialistic orators, and it was this verbal charm that gave your being a tense attraction. Why this sudden change?"

"No change, dear, in the root convictions of my life, nor in my pity for the poor of whom I'm still one. My position might have sobered me. With a new knowledge of men and things gained from a new angle, a realistic angle wherefrom the cloud of sentiments does not screen the dry light of the sky. For I see now clearly that life is so uneven and so numerous. Every step you take to save or lift another is but a step by which you crush some other, though it be very unwittingly. Like rain on rocks, it takes ages to polish a social order of peace and plenty to all, though it takes but three hours to blow the marble off to pieces. Only now I see all the sides of life, and see the better to carry to a triumphant close the ideas of our younger days. Give me a week, dear Rajee, I'll convince you; you will know me better then and judge me more charitably."

But Rajeswari was in a deep mood of contemplation.

In a throbbing voice Rangan said, with eyelids glued to eyes, "My life is void, my work is void, my heart is void, without you, Rajee. I'm but a heap of ashes without the spark of your breath. Promise me your love; let us both work together with courage and patience, as we planned at Oxford so often in dreamy hours of joy. Let us work from day to day, clear the filth of ages, giving the mute peasants a voice to speak with, a home to live in, and a zest in life they have never known, and an ever-widening vision of life and a cycle of joy. Only a Collector can do it all, if he but wishes. Dear Rajee, our words have always been rich in wisdom but we have always been poor in minting them into deeds of love and virtue; alas, for this our national trait! That is why we alone have lost our freedom among the nations of the world. Let us work in a humble way; work hard, detached and selfless, in the true *gita* way. And a collectorship is just the thing; a little kingship, wisely rendered, means the making of the beautiful lives of many millions. That is the great example to the world, I mean. Give me a week, Rajee. I'll convince you. You'll know me better then and judge me more charitably."

Rajeswari seemed to nod assent.

"I've a week's joining time—."

Rajeswari interrupted: "All that you say, Ranga is good when Swaraj is won and freedom for all is gained. You can never work for the poor, till the whole vicious system is changed. For, all our work in everyway and everywhere, even selfless work, goes now to feed only the few rich. Everything is so planned, marked, and channelled up. We must break these small, diverting, sinful, tragic bunds, and cut a new way. We must so order the new course that God's water flows equally to all the heads and fields. That is the real meaning of all this unrest, and the plan and purpose of these renascent times. You must play a part therein, Ranga, if you want me and my love. I've made up my mind. I'm going to work in the very district to which you now go out as Collector. Let the very hand which should tie the marital knot sentence me to prison—it is a rare pleasure, if such be God's will. But as you say, let us spend a week together and see the true way to work together. I agree."

"I've yet a week's joining time." The official slang gripped Rangan powerfully. "Rajee, let us go together to Tranquebar, the Queen of the Coromandel Coast. It is meet place for a fairy like you from the West. It's a beautiful spot for rest and thought."

Rajeswari nodded assent.

"Let us meet again to-night at the Egmore Railway Station at 8. The Boat Mail leaves at 8.30. I shall be waiting for you at the bottom step even from 7.45."

"Yes, I shall be there positively by 8."

Rangan shot a loving, lingering glance. And Rajee's eyes lingered lovingly for a while on Rangan's. A strange glow of pain quaked them. But liquid peace and strength shone through the tears that gathered therein—like dew-drops on lotus-buds.

CHAPTER III

THE TODDY-SHOP AT AKKUR

(1)

"KANDA, why are you so late to-day," shouted in one voice Nandan, Mookkan, and Katteri; Irullan, Karuppan, and Irullappan; and a straggling crowd of two dozens in different levels of drunkenness. They seemed for the moment to take more joy in Kandan's presence than in the sweet drink. For, Kandan was their saviour, their prop in the hour of need, the hero and saint of the place, who had come all the way from across the blue seas to reform them, to speak to them a gentle word of cheer, and supplement the verbal encouragement with a silver piece.

Even a drunkard has an illicit liking for a tee-totaller.

Kandan was in an unusually ruminating mood. Yes, there was saintliness in his face. He walked into the toddy-shop with a quick and calm gait instinctively commanding silence.

"Kanda, what's the matter with you to-day? We thought nothing ever went wrong with you, and you were a jolly, good fellow, ever smiling and sweet." Nallan asked with some deference. Even in putting this question he was a little more audacious than usual, for he had already finished three pots, and his eyes were rolling merry twinkles of laughter, and his speech changing to a child-like lisp of unuttered joy. He had taken only a sip from the fourth pot, but he flung it in high disdain as a mark of honor and sacrifice on Kandan's arrival. The unlucky pot rolled on, rolling and kneeling all the way till it got shelter under the knotted roots of a cocoanut tree.

" Nalla, havn't you heard the latest news of your lord?—you fine fellows with eyes and ears, but not using them except to find your way to this toddy-shop. I seem to help you but little to change your way of life. Havn't you heard of the latest?" Kandan cried repeating himself.

Finding his audience growing a little more attentive, he continued:

" Now, Mr. Mudaliar, foiled in his attempts to crush me himself with his own men, is begging the help of the *sircar*, the Police and the Collector, concocting wild tales against me to ruin me and my work. He'll find it no easy job to fight down the great cause of which I am but a servant, or the spirit of freedom that stirs the life of New India. I met your Mudaliar at the station waiting for No. 9, talking nicely to the new station master,—

a pale, withered, lean and hungry sort of fellow but blessed in a glorious wife, the like of whom in womankind for beauty and for majesty I have never seen on land or sea. Such flowers have been plucked from their garden in heaven like the *parijatam* and placed in the crowded market-places of earth for some divine, far-off purpose. She is like the stars that pelt the gloom of the sky with pebbles of light. There is such a thoughtful calm in her eyes as only sea-girt isles know in lonely mid-ocean. Our country needs such magnet souls for the great cause of our freedom. For, where words fail to persuade, the mere presence of such men and women does change the heart of millions and win the cause. May she become the Joan of Arc of Indian freedom !"

Kandan spoke more to himself inspired with a sense of liberation and eloquence which often a glimpse of a beautiful woman releases in a noble and dedicated mind. Kandan was stirred to the full joy of self-expression in the crowded loneliness of men who knew not this language of life. No woman had ever moved him more to a selfless joy. It was like the fall of snow on the Himalayan heights, a cloud-burst in the monsoon hour, or the wild beauty of a rushing river that breaks into a hundred cascades at some fateful turn of its young and intrepid life, only to flow again as a gentle river.

"Mr. Mudaliar, I saw it, was feeling a strange rebellion of the flesh when he rolled his heavy eyes all around the railway track, timid yet wanton, and rested them for a while at the station master's hut in which the lady was moving about, filling the window space with the glory of the morning sun. But, alas, Akkur, the deserted place of ancient Chola kings, I fear, will very soon enact a drama on the real stage of life and send a tragic cry of pain,—and with God's will I'll prevent at least the last act of the play."

Kandan paused a moment checking his own eloquence and its waste over these drunken fellows, cleared his throat, and began again :

"Mr. Mudaliar shot a fiery look of scorn at me. I answered it with a smile. It's for your sake, to work in my mother country, I came over here. I find life in our Tamil land, mean, dirty, and wretched beyond measure of words. In spite of all my active work for a year and more, you havn't improved a jot. Every evening I spend with you, and for a moment you seem to make up your mind that this shall be the last day of drink—only to break it the next evening."

(2)

Now Nandan, Mookkan, and Katteri, Irullan, Karuppan, and Irullappan slowly gathered round Kandan. Kandan drew a deep breath and continued in a changed tone after a slight pause.

"Now is the time for you, O Nanda, Irulla, and Nalla, to change your habits and make men of yourselves. Refuse to drink. Let us give up the toddy-shop and in its place erect a night school and I'll be proud to become your pial-teacher. Let Akkur set the example to the Tamil land. Refuse to work but for manly wages, give up this drink, and try to lead better lives every hour of the day. Mine has been so far a thankless task and all the money I've given you for useful work has but come stealthily into this toddy-shop. Nalla, I know you are both good and courageous. You are a born leader of men and the uncrowned king of the Akkur labour world. They may not listen to my voice. But these brave fellows you can lead to victory and set the example of a new life in the Tamil land. But the curse of drink is making you common clay with them, and cools your fire for the righteous things of life."

Kandan rose from his seat, and waving his hands said:

"Nalla, I feel in the air the rhythmic song of a changing order of life. Don't you hear even a distant hum of it? Awake, arise, now or never."

Kandan spoke with unusual vigor. He spoke passionately to ease the tension of his own fervent mood. Tears of pity at the fallen ways of his own men dimmed his eyes and closed them for a moment against the sad scenes of drink and revelry before him.

Nallan was touched. He stood up and made a solemn promise that he would become a reformed man.

"But, Kanda, as you yourself have said so often, the pity is we have to change the system as a whole and that only the rich and the powerful can do," Nallan began in a changed voice. "No doubt, you too are rich and powerful in your own land of Natal. But your strength is but a cow's strength against Mr. Mudaliar's, who is in his own element here like a crocodile in water. He is the chief man of the Taluq and the whole Government is his, and the whole social system clicks and sobs only as he winds the key."

"But, Nalla, you miss my purpose. You leave Mr. Mudaliar to his own ways. He will change with the general change. No man can shoot above or below his own atmosphere and live. Let us put our houses in order, cleanse ourselves and make that a pretty example to all. Try and see, courage and sacrifice can do how much for ourselves and our fellowmen. True sacrifice blesseth him that gives and him that takes. We'll never think or do evil to another. The great misery of life all around us here must disappear in another month and a new life of peace and plenty planned out for each and worked out by his own self-help. Or let me give up my life in this work."

Nallan replied in a low and husky voice, moved by the sincerity of Kandan: "Humble folk can never correct themselves or lead the way. The big men must do it. And you know Mr. Mudaliar is barely twenty-three and unmarried, has wasted himself at the most precious period. His aged mother weeps in vain at the truant ways of her son. The *pannaials* and agents are in arrears of wages now for several months; good work is not rewarded but bad counsel fed with royal bounty. And the greedy official world, from a petty peon to the Collector, fatten on him and they pat him on the back the wrong way. Already there's great discontent in the *pannai*. It would soon break into crime and arson. Hay-ricks and grain-heaps high as hillocks may catch fire in an angry moment and ungratefully burn to ashes."

Nandan, Mookkan, and Katteri, Irullan, Karuppan, and Irullappan began to cry "hurrah" shouting with the joy of approaching plunder. Katteri waved his long hands in support of the motion lifting them towards the star-lit fires of the sky.

Kandan, who listened to the whole speech very patiently, said in a very calm voice: "That way lies red ruin, ruin to all, ruin to my work, Nalla. It would profit neither, but only waste your own wealth, the food of the people. All my work has taught you only this!"

"But that's the only way known to us, poor, ignorant, toiling folk. Ask these fellows, if you please to verify my words."

"Hip, hip, hurrah!" shouted all in one voice, Nandan, Mookkan, and Katteri, Irullan, Karuppan, and Irullappan. "We'll do it to-day; master is away."

Everyone raised his hands as if ready to act at once and cried, "We'll do it to-day, master is away."

"No, no, Nalla, that's simply exciting these poor fellows to their own ruin. Peace begets peace; war begets war."

"Look yonder by the mango tree. Karian is coming," Nallan shouted. "He is the spy set on you by Mr. Mudaliar to plot your ruin."

(3)

Karian was seen coming slowly with measured, strident steps and extra joy in his looks. Kandan watched him with intent care and received him with a sweet smile and open arms.

"Karia, you'll live a hundred years," cried Irullappan whose deep malice, drink only made more palpable. He, who passed this benediction on Karian, took always a beneficent interest in promoting the feud between Kandan and Karian.

"Yes, I knew from your looks that you were talking of me—and talking ill of me. What else could it be when my cousin, Kandan, is here stirring gentleness to revolt, and good work to destruction, always letting a spark of fire on hay-ricks and grain-heaps? Yes, dry fellows are prone to mischief. That's why I've always commended him to a drink to make a man of him, that he may see the light of life clearly, even as we see it through this milky vision of glory." Karian pointed out with pride a potful of the foaming white juice, and thought of the contents in his hand with the prospective pleasure of annexation. Karian spoke with a rare moderation and a suppressed glee in his voice.

"What is the good luck of the day that makes you so eloquent and cheerful, Karia?" asked Nallan.

Karian flung open his palm, and five silver rupees shone with amazing lustre. He turned with an inward chuckle towards Kandan.

Kandan and Karian were first cousins. Their fathers were brothers of a joint Hindu family. Their ancestral home was at Tillayadi, a progressive village with a thousand houses. Karian's father was the elder of the two and ruled the family with an iron hand. He had seen better days under the Danish Government. In fact, he had led in his younger days a faction so successfully that the Danish Governor at Tranquebar was obliged to appoint him the chief magistrate of the place. The iron rule of the elder brother chafed the free and roaming spirit of the younger, Kandan's father, Nallappan, who fled to Natal one day when the rebellious mood was high. He had then hardly completed twenty-four. But that age was always reckoned as the critical year for a youth in Nallappan's family when fortune was made or marred.

Nallappan's record of humble and devoted work in the passive resistance movement in Natal under the leadership of Mahatma Gandhi is the record of work of all unknown volunteers in the struggle for justice and freedom. It is rarely chronicled in the books of men but has always the first place in the scroll of the recording angel.

And the age of twenty-four proved really critical to Kandan as well. He was a student at Oxford, and passed brilliantly the I.C.S. examination. He met with a reverse in the very hour of victory in an affair of the heart. Disappointed love in the pregnant hour of change destroyed the self and changed itself into the higher love for all beings. Kandan voluntarily threw up the assured and kingly career of an Indian Civil Servant at the probation period. He finally decided to settle down in his own Tamil land and do some public work. Therefore, he came over to India, to his own village of Tillayadi. His arrival synchronised with the construction of a railway track to his own place and it seemed to him of happy augury. Kandan learnt that Karian was the sole surviving member of his family and of the low state into which it had fallen.

As for Karian, with the transfer of the Government from the Danish to the British, Karian's father rapidly declined in influence and wealth, in position and emoluments. He died a broken-hearted man leaving behind him to Karian only a few acres of sand-dunes, wind-swept and dry.

The first act of Karian was to sell away these precious three acres of sand-dunes, and look about for an investment which gave him some initiative and scope for his strength and industry. Fortunately the new railway line from Mayavaram to Tranquebar was being laid and it was greatly exercising the mind of the people. Karian tried his fortune as an earth-work contractor with the modest capital of five hundred rupees, his all.

The one conspicuous quality of the Kandan-Karian family was a chronic inability to adjust themselves to changing situations. Karian did his contract work with great uprightness but lost his all in the job, because he failed to please the army of officials that hung on to him like dog-flies over a honey-comb.

But Karian remained undaunted. He took a vow before his family Goddess Brihannayaki at Tillayadi and the famous Mariamman at Olugumangalam that he would somehow make good his money from this very railway line. He had enough following of *budmashes* in his own village to hold up a night train and smash the few old coaches for the sheer joy of it, and pilfer the passengers for what they were worth. But this seemed, in the broad daylight of the twentieth century, even to Karian in his splendid and predatory youth, a little ungainly and antiquated affair.

Karian could get only the job of a porter-pointsman at Akkur, which on first thoughts he was for declining as quite menial. He had even decided to sail away to Natal like his revered uncle. But a bird in the hand was worth two in the bush—somebody said—and Karian learnt at least so much out of his railway contract. And he was encouraged that the portership, though menial and degrading, had its own scheduled perquisites and possibilities. And true to his vow he began to milk money from every rustic with a seeming load of excess luggage. Karian was an expert at weighing and the poor folk got alarmed at the mere sight of the weighing machine with its dacoit 'arm' projecting from its very mouth, and pointing accusingly at every passer-by.

Kandan strove his best to be on very friendly terms with Karian, and in fact viewed him as a possible helpful collaborator in his schemes of national uplift and amelioration. Kandan admired the dash and energy, the courage and quickness, and the wonderful popularity of Karian. But Karian met him like brushwood meeting fire. He felt keenly his low position in life, and his agnatic blood boiled over with jealousy.

Kandan however never failed in his efforts, when the chance came, to make up with Karian, especially as he felt that he was the sole surviving member of his family, and that his joys and sorrows should but rightly be shared with him. He offered him his love, his money, his person, and everything, to please Karian and win him over for ever. But Karian found his pride and poverty so far the chief obstacles in the way.

But on this occasion Karian seemed to be in a very pleasant humour. Kandan summoned up his very best and stretched out his right hand to Karian. This offer of fellowship he implemented with appropriate looks and gestures.

Karian's triumphal income of five rupees that day really bridged the agnatic gulf and decided the issue.

"Yes, Kanda, made up. Dear cousin, will you celebrate this occasion with a sip of this sweet drink of the gods? Taste it but once, you would leave off preaching against this nectar! And we could be friends and cousins for ever."

Kandan smiled his most gracious and disarming smile, the smile of a child pure and innocent, and kept silent, lest words uttered at random should spoil the peace-effects.

Karian opened his palm, and five rupees of shining silver beamed. Everyone cried, "hurrah." Karian flung the rupees to the salesman and exclaimed, "Let us celebrate the occasion with a free drink to all our friends and fellows."

There was an hour of revelry in the toddy-shop on an unprecedented scale.

Kandan gently hinted to Karian that it was perhaps time for him to go home for meal and be ready to receive in time No. 13 from Tranquebar.

Kandan and Karian soon parted after a fond fraternal embrace, vowing eternal loyalty to each other in the name of their great-grandfather.

But in the toddy-shop the spirit ran very high as soon as the moral check of Kandan's presence was removed. There .was much merry singing and laughing, screaming and shouting, in as many grades of intoxication as the purse of each and the gift of Karian would allow. Even the placid tank seemed to share in it, with merry ripples riding on to the shore and breaking at the very feet of these drunken men. In the general uproar of the toddy-shop Katteri's voice was heard the loudest, urging the men to the quickening joy of plunder that very night.

Nandan, Mookkan, Katteri, Irullan, Karuppan and Irullappan shouted approval clapping their hands.

Five rupees' worth ot free drink is a windfall of the first magnitude to these poor tillers of the soil. And the toddy-shop wore the look of festal gaiety of Indra's own palace hall of pleasure in Heaven.

CHAPTER IV

TO BE OR NOT TO BE

(1)

PADMA was a soft-skinned, sweet-tempered, lotus-eyed lad of seventeen. He was the last born of a family of numerous fifteen, in which the daughters definitely predominated over the sons, indicating something of the virile share which Neelakshi had thrown into the conjugal partnership. But the daughters had a splendid success in the matrimonial market. For Neelakshi had succeeded not only in the mere minor triumph of transmitting her sex but also in reproducing in her daughters her glorious complexion and refined features. The far-seeing mother had bestowed on this lovely bunch of daughters infinite patience in the rearing and disposing of them. Calm and vigilant in the most intricate transactions of marriage she always won the best of a wide range of suitors. Till she actually chose her son-in-law she kept all of them hopeful and dreaming.

But Neelakshi found the upbringing of her sons a more difficult job. Her husband came of a family long ago settted on land. But she gave up the ancestral village in favour of Shiyali, a semi-urban centre, fortunately blessed with a railway station at which all trains stopped except the Boat Mail. All her five sons ran up to the matriculation class. Some negotiated the minor hurdles of class promotions at least the second time. But all of them found the matriculation examination too wide and disastrous a ditch for their jumping power.

The shrewd mother understood that she had not succeeded in transmitting her own quality to her sons. She deplored the lack of talent and ambition, alas, of the sons sprung of her own loins. A subtle reaction evidently pervaded the natal hour and withheld the classic qualities of the mother from her own sons. But Raghu, the last but one and the elder to Padma, was an exception to this reaction of quality in the male progeny. She knew Padma as an exception almost by natural insight and so she persevered with him and gave him her best.

Neelakshi had so far succeeded in scattering her failed matriculates and S. S. L. C.s all over the Tamil districts—for she was fruitful over a wide period of time which the progressive University of Madras had beneficently used to experiment with the course of studies for the young. She had succeeded in securing for some, mainly with the help of her sons-in-law, minor jobs of clerkships in public offices and private firms. And some others not so good even for such jobs she had wisely settled as part of the *pannai* of her richer sons-in-law who showed a melting tenderness for the affiliated blood.

(2)

Raghu really displayed great promise. He passed his S. S. L. C., the first in his high school at the first attempt. He read history with a discerning eye to the large movements of ideas that shaped human events, and specialised in Economics and Labour problems as subjects of increasing importance in world's affairs especially in India's unshapen future. He successfully graduated but missed very narrowly a first class in the University though he scored one in life by his marriage. In the final collegiate year his impoverished mother had to marry Raghu to an irrigation engineer's daughter solely with a view to avoid a financial break down. This happy event distracted Raghu's attention from his studies with its *deepavali* travels and presents and all the unrest which matrimony means at that tender age. That was the only mistake Neelakshi ever committed in her long and busy life but she was obliged to do so to replenish her treasury. Except for a dilapidated house in the ancestral village, the family at this time owned nothing on earth. But thanks to this fortunate alliance it brought in three thousand rupees of the irrigation engineer's over stocked gold—Raghu was sold at one hundred times his share of the inheritance value.

Raghu with his resources so providentially supplemented tried indeed very hard for the I. C. S. He went up to Delhi with conscious pomp by the Grand Trunk Express—he was far surer of his administrative capacity than of his academic talents —but failed of course for want of a few marks to get into the chosen arc. Then he tried several offices for a job till he had nearly run out the three thousands. And he quietly settled down to journalism which, thank God, required no capital except a pennyworth of ink and paper and of course postage to and fro to carry safely its own weight. Out of three dozens he conceived and wrote in the highest moments of his creative fancy only three got locally published though he sent all of them abroad with amazing perseverance to the very ends of the earth, London to New York, New York to California. One of the three happened to be a laudatory research article on the economic and labour organisation in Vedic times. The local Deputy Collector happened to be similarly engaged in such research as a recreation from the exactions of civil and criminal administration and as a reaction to a promotion long over due but denied. He wrote appreciatively of the maiden efforts of the young man and gave intelligent and elderly advice on the proper lines of research and as an allied subject for collateral study suggested the Sumerian civilisation.

The young graduate, Raghu, enthusiastically responded to the generous words of praise, and sent in the next day an application for a clerkship at the earnest entreaty of Neelakshi not to miss the chance but to make hay while the sun shines. There was fortunately a vacancy in the Taluq office of Shiyali, and the Deputy Collector warm and intellectual by temperament defied the standing orders that no Brahmin should be appointed to a clerkship in the Division until further orders blessed Raghu with an appointment that carried initially twenty-five rupees a month and the baton of the field marshall in the knapsack. Raghu may still become a Collector some day though just now crawling on the bottom rung.

There were no bounds to the joy at home that day. Neelakshi was overjoyed; for some monthly income was a dire necessity as her daughter-in-law had already come home with a boy of five and a girl of two in the cradle. Raghu sincerely took to his slaving work at the desk for all his juvenile ambition, and became a happy breadwinner of the family. A few months rolled on and Raghu continued steadily his honest grind of revenue accounts.

And Padma, the last born was in the sixth form preparing or supposed to prepare for the S. S. L. C., public examination. Padma's forefathers were village magistrates before Neelakshi's driving ambition and fertility drove the family to the adventures of town life. The hereditary taste for public affairs which expressed itself in Raghu in his passionate attachment to Economics and Labour problems had a precocious outburst in Padma in patriotic song and deeds.

Padma, the lotus-eyed, for all his softness of features and kindly expression was a born rebel whom the time-spirit and a wooden system of education had kindled to quick flame. And the youngest in a joint Hindu family is either a born rebel or a slave of all work. On the inheritance side he gets nothing as everything movable and immovable is exhausted by his elders before he sees the light of day or attains the age of discretion to commit indiscretions. And his boyhood nominally owning allegiance to school is more or less a period of menial service to the elders who boss over him.

Padma began to take recognition of this ill-jointed world very early in life. The unrest of the decade hatched him into a precocious public worker. Padma took to the *Hindu* newspaper and the patriotic meetings on the uppanar sands like duck to water where ears of corn lay floating. His text-books, what few he had purchased, he had long ago sent down the temple tank to consecrate some patriotic vow he had taken for public service. Still he kept on attending school just to gain those qualities of leadership which he hoped would stand him in good stead in later life.

Still for all his truancy to his studies Padma was easily successful in school. He regularly passed his class examinations without any sort of industry to the amazement of his own teachers. So Padma was cocksure of success, for all his devotion to public work as a full time local worker who met and garlanded at the station even at midnight every provincial and national hero who passed that way by any train except the Boat Mail which did not stop there but for whose stopping Padma had already sent a monster petition to the Agent and the Railway Board at New Delhi.

Padma reckoned the selection examination by the headmaster as a tyrannical and wasteful diversion and mockery, and did it in a very perfunctory way. Still he hoped to pass the S. S. L. C., public examination by sitting up a few days before the ordeal, borrowing the books of so many rich lads who kept the books tidy for the next year sure to fail this time. Raghu chided Padma for his patriotic vagrancy, and Padma mocked at Raghu, the distinguished student of economics and labour problems, for the slave's work at the desk twelve hours a day, all too sterile for words or tears.

The Time-spirit of Renascent India played tragically through every nook and corner of life like a cyclone in its windiest hour before the rains.

(3)

It was a Saturday evening—the same evening in which we witnessed the events chronicled in the foregoing chapters.

Neelakshi was busy negotiating the price of a bundle of firewood which an old woman of the *irulla* caste was hawking in the streets for sale. Neelakshi with her sure business instinct knew how to negotiate successfully at rock-bottom rates with these poor and hungry vendors. Raghu had promised to return rather early for lunch that day and she was eargerly waiting for him to give him, hot and crisp, a few *uthappams* with a dainty ball of fresh butter riding over them. The fire-wood was knocked down at less than the cost of labour for splitting the wood. Raghu came home and had a really nice lunch with his mother all alone.

Padma was busy in the streets of Shiyali,—he had not had even his breakfast at home,—gathering the vagrant lads up for a monster procession and a meeting of protest against some ill-conceived act of the Government of India and the support which the Secretary of State for India gave it in a speech at a luncheon given in his honour in London. Neelakshi's maternal bosom heaved a sigh of pain at the thought that Padma was not there to share in the domestic lunch.

"Raghu, you are becoming more and more indifferent to your home affairs, more and more absorbed in your official work. Padma is fast getting adrift—truant and reckless. You should check him immediately or the boy will be lost to us in the Gandhian flood."

"I should check him, mother!—and get a slap in the face! Already he is advising me to kick off my job and respond to the country's call,—and that God would feed us all as he feeds the sparrow. He is an unruly colt, mother, though he looks so soft and speaks so soft. The blood of the rebel is in him. You alone should try to check him, your youngest,—and your dearest." Raghu finished with a significant laugh.

"Yes, Raghu, I'm partly to blame—at least now I'll give him a bit of my mind. For all his wildness, I trust, he will pull through the S.S.L.C.—and also the selection examination held last week. We've to pay his examination fees in a day or two as soon as the headmaster puts up the list—and I've not a pie on hand—I've tried all sources open to me and failed. Can you manage it, Raghu, in the office from your fellow-clerks."

"Manage it from my fellow-clerks!—shrivelled-up, old, battered affairs who daily depend on me and the *karnams* for a copper or two for their *pan* and snuff. I may as well ask the *tahsildar* for a loan!"

"Then, Raghu, there must be many rich *mirasdars* whom you must have helped in many ways—will they not help you with such a trifling sum as this?"

"That way surely, mother, red ruin lies, and it is dishonest. It would make my sweated and slaved food, mother, doubly repugnant."

"Only a loan I suggest, Raghu, not a bribe."

"It's impossible, mother. No such distinction exists in the official world."

Already the shouts of boys in multitudes and in moving procession were heard at the western end of the street corner. For, Padma had succeeded in declaring a school strike for the afternoon to protest in a monster meeting assembled on the sands of uppanar against the action of the Government of India. And Padma bravely laid the route of the procession along his own street so that his mother might have a glimpse of the infant power that he was already in local affairs and in the country's cause. He led the boys with banner in hand singing to himself a tune slightly different from the patriotic chorus-song of the crowd. Neelakshi's heart was filled with both pride and anger.

Neelakshi openly called out for Padma in the crowd and scolded him vigorously for his wild, wasteful and unruly life, and spoke in a sharp voice of decision which she alone could command, a voice which was already fretting with the thought of lack of funds for the many vital needs of home life.

"I'm sure, Padma, you will fail in the examination, and it is a mere waste to send you up even if you chance to get into the selection list. Don't enter my house, so long as you lead this reckless and vagrant life."

The sensitive lad Padma stopped the tune he was singing to himself and shouted at the top of his voice, "All right, mother, I shall not enter your house, pass or fail. Be happy with Raghu. The call of the country calls me away from home." His mother's words were a chastisement administered before a crowd, and his words, an oath of honour taken in an excited but sacred hour, taken in the presence of so many. It went deep into the sensitive mind of Padma.

(4)

It was an excited, crowded, unprecedentedly crowded, patriotic meeting that the boys held on the sands of uppanar under the leadership of Padma. Raghu, his brother, was almost the only young man of his age in Shiyali who did not attend this monster meeting. There were as many as five speeches in English and seven in Tamil and one in Hindi for the unity of India. Padma who presided spoke first in English, then in Tamil, then in Hindi, broken but expressive. He scattered pellmell all through his speeches quotations from Sanskrit especially from the Bhagavad-Gita in support of his protest against the action of the Government of India.

The juvenile president had hardly closed the peroration of his fervid speech in English when a smart young lieutenant of his ran up to him and whispered into his ears, "I hear the selection results have just been published, Padma, and your name is not there, nor mine! What shall we do?"

Padma did not lose his presence of mind. He courageously stood up and said to the boys in the meeting, "Before we dissolve this meeting I have to announce you to-day that the selection list has just been published and that the headmaster has cut down fifty per cent of us, including myself. We have just been protesting against the high-handed action of the Viceroy and the Government of India, and we should from now turn our attention to local affairs. Meanwhile let us go in a body and find out the facts."

Yes, they marched on to the school in crowded excitement under the leadership of Padma. They saw the list with perspiring eagerness. But it was a slender one of three in which Padma ranked first. Even his lieutenant who gave the news was not in the list. The other two were notorious slackers, sons of local magnates, who went to school because they had fine clothes to wear and were too troublesome at home.

In five minutes Padma found he became a leper. One by one all his friends who applauded his eloquence but half an hour ago till land and water echoed to the juvenile shouts melted away quietly. He found himself reeling on the parallel bars for support almost all alone on the school playground. He was lost in thought for five minutes. But he quickly recovered himself as he thought of his mother and brother at home and the evening incident. He hastened towards the railway station side by the back exit of the school along a short cut by the side of an irrigation channel, unnoticed by anybody. Nearing the station he heard the Parcel Express thundering on the fateful uppanar bridge. That settled his plan of future action. It was his first failure in life. The sensitive lad smarted under it. He took it to heart. But he gained the true taste of life from his first failure.

(5)

The Parcel Express came slowly steaming into the platform carrying as if with conscious pride its mixed load of perishables and imperishables ; fruits, vegetables, and men. Padma had always a weird fancy for the steam engine as the very emblem of the glory of motion, and looked upon the station-yard as a place of the keenest pleasure for the study of men and women in the most liquid condition of their lives, and often longed, at the bottom of his juvenile heart for the longest journeys. But this evening he did not feel the ecstasy of motion but felt a prisoner in the open space of the platform and the throng of men.

Just when the train whistled to start he slipped into one of the crowded compartments, and put out his head just to see who was the white trousered gentleman who got into the next carriage. He could not see him though he craned his neck very hard but heard the gruff voice of the ticket examiner calling for tickets. Padma had done many a time with his gay band of boys joyous free rides to the Coleroon in the same Parcel Express. But this time his heart strangely clicked alarm, and he felt that he was diminishing by inches almost to the vanishing point.

Padma had made up his mind to slip out of the train on the wrong side at the next station of Coleroon, and await the chances by another train. Padma effected his escape safely. Quickly walking across the rails he gained the shelter of the darkness of the giant avenue trees growing rankly on the rich alluvial soil. The goods-shed lay like a masouleum a little beyond.

A strange thought stole through his mind for the first time, "What is the worth of my life to me or to my fellows? Let me end it quietly in the glory of the Coleroon floods and reach the everlasting sea in half an hour." A fat, wild lizard clicked 'amen' from among the stored bags of paddy in the goods-shed, and a huge tree lizard murmured assent from amidst the dark leafy branches of a giant tree.

The gloom seemed to become darker, and at the mysterious prophetic voice of the lizard, Padma shuddered a little more and moved along the rails to the open sky towards the Coleroon bridge, soliloquising with a maturity which three hours of grief and failure had already given him, "I'm but one of fifteen to my mother, and why this wild profusion?

It seems God has but wantonly made me only for waste. Let me carry out His wish; and my mother won't miss me; drown myself in the mighty river after one splendid ecstasy of swimming. None loves a bath in roaming waters dearer than myself and it is a fitting close to my career; let me have the longest swim and the sweetest death;—and the sea throw up as feed for the vultures on the shore the body from which life had been taken out by the human vultures on the land; and perchance my ghost may haunt the soul, the sleeping and the waking hours of my headmaster."

A new courage came to him with this resolve. With firm steps he marched on balancing himself lightly on the shining rails as if he were a trained trolley puller.

The magnificent Coleroon was but a furlong off the station. The rumbling sound of the Parcel Express thundering along the massive iron bridge had not yet died down. It but seemed to cheer the pedestrian Padma to run along its wake and feel the joy of it for himself.

Padma balancing himself on the shining rails sped like a serpent along the lawn. He bet within himself that if he chanced to slip off the rails, he would surely die. Strange to say though he wanted to drop off he could not. Some magnet glow at his heels kept him to the shining rails. He did not and could not slip off. What a strange thing destiny is? He was so unhelpably alive even for a merry puzzle! So like a trolley-man he flew on the edge of the shining rails till he reached the wonderland of the river and the bridge. He saw the river by the crescent moonlight not in the glory of floods but in the greater glory of sand, with deep pools of clear water here and there.

Padma spoke to himself: "Are the pools deep enough to drown me?"

"Is Padma to leave his tender body floating in a stagnant pool against the gay morning sun. No, no. To be drowned in the Coleroon in floods has at least the glorious end of a roiling sea. No, Padma never will die in a pond like a stoned frog."

He was already a few yards up on the railway bridge. He sat on the massive end of the third pier, looked on the glory of the river-bed bathed in crescent moonlight, and said to himself, "The river has cheated me of my resolve. Why not sleep over the rails forever and leave a mangled tender corpse just to illustrate the story of man's misdeeds on earth once again?"

Before the thought could mature into a firm resolve, Padma felt a native repugnance to this form of death. And all too soon a goods train came blazing its searchlight along the track. It seemed a difficult job for Padma to face death before such publicity. He became undecided as the train drew nearer, grinding and whistling. He jumped over the bridge at the last moment as a compromise in conflict between life and death, courage and cowardice and fell sheer eighteen feet below into a deep pool, splashing the quiet water to showering heights. It was indeed very deep and a little broad. Padma knew swimming as well as a fish. How could he get drowned for all his wish in a stagnant pool? He swam ashore briskly, walked back in deep sand to the high banks of the river, fell into a deep reverie. The cool bath refreshed his fevered brain and pulsed it to clearer thoughts of the joy of living. It cut a change for him from the immediate past.

An hour later Padma stood up and prostrated himself to the Unseen God once, twice, thrice, and stood up again transfixed in prayer for over half an hour with his palm joined to palm.

"I'll catch the Ceylon Boat Mail, and at Colombo get into one of the Australian steamers, hiding myself in the coal-bunks, even as Lord Reading did; return ten years hence to India if not as the Viceroy, at least as a pioneer with funds for a new system of education and of life—at any rate, having reached an age when none would ever think of putting me to school again."

So with this deep resolve Padma waited at the Coleroon station for the Ceylon Boat Mail from Madras, hiding himself and his aching but active, dreaming youth behind the big banyan trees, listening to the prophetic voice of a lizard now and then and trying to interpret it in his own favour.

CHAPTER V

FIRST CLASS FOR LUGGAGE AND THIRD CLASS FOR MEN

(1)

TRUE to his word, Rangan arrived at the Egmore station in a high grade Buick Taxi. He had already booked in the morning his journey to Tranquebar taking a First Class ticket. In a fit of modesty he gave his name as plain " R. S. Rangaswami " on the reservation card. He purposely withheld the magic letters " I.C.S." as he had a feeling that without the trappings of office his personality would not come up to the ordinary requirements of his designation. He now travelled alone even without a *chokra*. For the worship of Rajee must be done in splendid isolation with a consecrated mind.

But Rangan was not totally devoid of personality. True, he had not a fine presence, a fair complexion and a symmetrical and stately build. But he had a kind of racy intellectual expression whose magnetism was felt by those who could respond to it, a very cultured few. This was the chief quality which attracted Rajeswari to Rangan in a foreign land.

It was as a socialistic preacher that Rangan found his full stature, and his ardent love of socialism acted also as a preliminary incentive to a keener study of the I.C.S. curricula. For it helped him to plumb in some measure the degrading depths of human misery which a tilted social system insures for the many that it may benefit the few. Hence it was no wonder that he had the magic, suffusing glow of sincerity which all born orators develop at the tip of their tongue like the fireless light the glow-worm does at the tail.

Otherwise Rangan looked a very common man, dark in complexion, awkward and shuffling in gait, tall and thin, with an ungainly but distinguished countenance. But it was his voice that had the redeeming gift. Its timbre was sweet and attractive. It had a converting touch. But these are qualities not felt at the first sight but only in the intimacies of conversation. So Rangan, now no more an orator but an administrative head bedecked with red tape and flag, felt the need, to assert and proclaim his dignity, of belted peons and the flowing toga robes of attendants who went about in front fussing and hissing. For Rajeswari Bai's sake he hurried to Madras all alone lost in sweet unrest and reverie.

The moment Rangan reached the portico for first and second class passengers, he was besieged by a ragged army of porters. He had developed of late a decided habit for heavy luggage, though in his student days he was famous for travelling light—in fact except for the *dhoti* he wore, he had nothing surplus to carry home for the vacation. The Egmore third-class entrance was full of such vivid memories. But he quickly turned away from this plebeian scene of his earlier years of struggle and poverty. Of course the ragged army of porters was unaware of the august presence of the Assistant Collector.

Rangan, who knew very well how to organise and present the case of a Trade Union of porters if the call came, knew nothing of the highly skilled and diplomatic negotiations required to settle with these hungry men a reasonable charge for entraining his luggage. He stood puzzled ; besieged by the clamours of a battered and vociferous army of unemployed. He had matters of importance weighing heavily on his mind. Meanwhile for every little bag, like ants to a drop of honey, came running, in crowded confusion, porters, black and fair, young and old, moustached and clean-shaven. Everyone took hold of an article unceremoniously, claiming special appointment, some by virtue of a gesture, some by a wink of the master's eye, and some, more audacious than the rest, by express call by name.

Rangan found it impossible to quell this riot of co-operation and resigned himself to his fate which would after all mean but a rupee more to these poor fellows. Were not his early socialistic doctrines worth at least that much at this critical hour ?

Porters are generally a shrewd lot, taught in the rough school of railway station life with its variety of experience, from generosity to meanness, from sterling honesty to vile trickery. They could easily weigh a man's heart and ascertain his intentions quicker and more accurately than the weighing machine could do his luggage. They found out Rangan's name and class; he had already been spotted in the morning as a possible prey and his pedigree traced sufficiently for their purposes, except for the I.C.S., for which there was no warrant about him. His luggage safely found its way to the first-class berth assigned to him. But Rangan's transit seemed less easy.

(2)

Rangan was faced with a real problem. Rajeswari Bai was travelling and he must find for her a berth along with him. He regretted that he had not used in the morning the magic letters "I.C.S." Now to declare to the railway menials that he was an I.C.S., just to secure another berth was to court an enquiry and cheapen the prestige of his own peerless Service.

So the Asst. Collector in mufti approached the ticket-collector on duty at the entrance to the platform, who stood at ease with a serenity and sourness patented only in railway service, and asked him very gently, "May I see the station master?"

"No, you can't see him," came the abrupt reply like a shot from a toy air-gun.

"Can't?"

"Can't. I say you can't. He's very busy."

"May I go in?"

"Yes, if you have a platform ticket—one anna please, put a nickel-piece in the slot and pull out a ticket this way." The ticket-collector encouraged his words of eloquence with such a significant smile and twinkle of the eye as to suggest that the nickel-piece might well be saved the obscurity of the steel-box and given the publicity of his own palm.

Rangan searched his pocket for a nickel-piece but found only a four-anna silver bit. "I haven't a nickel-piece, collector. But here's a four-anna bit, silver. Please have't."

Rangan slipped the coin with a faint smile and a gentle finger tip. The ticket-collector understood the kindness, and took the silver piece stealing a glance all over. It was the revealing, piteous glance of the under-dog whom civilisation sweats so that the lords of the earth may fly like angels at forty miles an hour. The dog licks the fleshless bone and its tail wags with the joy which an unkind but resurgent memory kindles. The ticket-collector became gracious all at once.

"Very well, sir, please come in. I'm at your service. The stationmaster is a big man. You can't easily get at him. I'll help you. Please tell me your difficulties. Haven't you heard of the proverb, sir, the *karnam* can help you better than the Collector?"

"Thanks, what's your name—and pay, ticket-collector?"

"My name is Rangaswami and friends call me Rangan. And my pay is twenty-five rupees, sir, and I'm a family man with five daughters and three sons, and it's very hard work here, sir, as you know."

"Yes, indeed, I quite see your point. Just help me a little. I've taken a first class to Tranquebar by the Boat Mail."

"First class to Tranquebar!—then why a platform ticket, sir? I'm so sorry—."

"It doesn't matter at all, a few annas, ticket-collector. I want another berth in the same compartment. A lady is now travelling with me, and I must find her a seat somehow. Will you kindly arrange?"

Rangan's voice grew tender and confused with anxiety. His temperament was academic and not practical. He rejoiced in words and reveries. He was frayed and annoyed at the prospect of having to do things. He suffered a strange agony.

"I'm glad you have come a little early. I'll do my best and let you know in five minutes."

Rangan, the Assistant Collector, slipped a rupee into the spacious palm of the ticket-collector whose grateful fingers closed in joy on the rupee with a falcon's speed. The ill-pared nails scratched on the thin skin of the true Collector, a trail of comradeship in the hour of need and service, and established a real union of hearts between the two collectors.

The news spread everywhere kindling to activity the under-dogs of the railway station even as a drop of honey attracts a crowd of ants and flies.

The Boat Mail has always a crowded traffic. There was no extra first-class berth available that night to manipulate easily. But soon it was found that a fat Chetti, a banker, was registered to travel first in the same compartment. He belongs to a class of people who are always easy material to negotiate with in matters where vague, fundamental rights that cannot be reduced to money value are concerned. It was at once decided, of course *ex parte*, by the menial railway gods that he should either travel second class by the Boat Mail or first class by the next train which left an hour later. The Chetti gladly acquiesced in this arrangement, and forgot the pain of travel in the reverie of accumulating interest in three countries and thirty districts.

For, money-lenders are usually the meekest in the world though they are the most courageous and persistent in matters calling for affidavits. For, usury kills the red corpuscles in the blood, and increases the deposit of fat very near the heart. If the good luck of a parasite is rich and easy food, it is paid for by the total destruction of the first quality of life, courage.

The Chetti who arrived clear half an hour earlier than Rangan was solemnly appraised of the difficulties in the way of his travelling first class, as a *dorai* wanted to travel in the same compartment with a lady. The final choice was put before him: the second class or the next train?

The Chetti readily consented, saying humbly, "First or second is the same to me, sir. I travel first for the sake of prestige—a little place in any corner of the Boat Mail, I pray, will do for me. I've to attend to-morrow my grand-daughter's marriage and the second train goes too late for the function."

(3)

Rangan was overjoyed with the return for his rupee. Happy and fluttering, everything ready, he was waiting eagerly at the portico, craning his neck and drying his eyes to sight Rajeswari Bai. He fancied he was already rolling at forty miles an hour in the luxurious first-class of the Boat Mail with Rajee by his side. Meanwhile every hooting car that came grinding to the flight of steps raised his hopes. Time fleeted painfully, and his eyes dimmed with disappointment. Still only fifteen minutes left! Rajee was not the woman to break her word or change her mind!

He thought he heard her voice emerging from the crashing din and hellish noise at the entrance to the third-class gate, where a raging crowd was fighting for every inch of standing space as if in trench warfare. He quickly ran up to her: yes, it was Rajeswari herself.

Rajeswari Bai came by bus which ran late as it burst its tyre on the way near the Royapettah hospital, when it leisurely canvassed for custom inviting every passer-by. On her arrival, even the few things she carried, a little bag and a small bed, were annexed without her consent and without any ceremony by a crowd of porters who came yelling like wolves. They quarrelled now among themselves as to who first touched the luggage, and gained the right to carry; always a difficult point to decide even after full evidence in the case: for hungry hands fly to their food at the same velocity.

Rangan was delighted. "That's not the way, Rajee. It is the wretched third-class entrance, the same as ever, a little hell on earth in India. Here it is—our way to the first-class. I've booked first for both of us."

The Assistant Collector with an air of authority turned towards the shouting, unruly porters who had not yet decided the subtle question of who touched first. "I'll cane you, rascals, you feller there, take up the things," and Rangan pointed to a broad-shouldered Atlas who had just come to see what the matter was for so much excitement even in a railway station. The last called was once again the first chosen.

"No, no, Ranga, I carry my own things,—not very many. Besides I'm travelling third." There was decision in her voice and eyes.

"Travelling third, hell—it is here, Rajee. It is not England, Rajee; third class is worse than cattle-pen ; it is hell ; slime, spit and filth. Travelling third, you who filled the P. & O. boats with your royal luggage and trunks ; you who travelled first-class in a first-class ocean-liner, to travel third in the S.I.R. ! Are you mad, Rajee ? You'll suffocate yourself. I have booked first-class for both of us."

Rangan entreated her in vain. Rajeswari did not move an inch. "I'm travelling third, no doubt about it. If you want my company, run up and take two third-class tickets to Tranquebar."

Rajeswari stood firm and calm, shining in the crowd like the moon through the small openings in a dark cloud.

(4)

But getting a third-class ticket at the Egmore station is itself an acrobatic feat which some enterprising firm may well roll into a motion picture for the joy of the world, of course, after paying for the film rights to the South Indian Railway. Rangan knew well the nature of the difficult work, and remembered the agility of his younger days to glide like an eel through sweating masses of men.

Just in front of the third-class booking-office window stands a stately revolving iron cage six feet high, divided into four folds. One should pass through this cage to secure a ticket.

There was already a heaving, raging, cursing, sweating crowd of old and young, struggling for their way to the coveted cage that issued the pass to Heaven. The lord of tickets sat on the other side careless of the woes of mankind—amidst heaps of silver and copper pieces thrown into hollow discs, mounding up like a pyramid. He seemed a veteran of seventy summers. His *namam* was faint, being wet with the oiled perspiration of ages. He had long ago ceased to wipe off this running brook as it proved to be a perennial stream. He was sick of the familiar, toiling crowd before him, and recently he had calamities of his own. His daughter was widowed, and he applied for leave which could not be granted as no relieving hand suitable to such a big station as Egmore was available. Just the previous night in the Boat Mail issue he had lost one rupee, eight annas and three pies. The thought of the loss still racked him, for it meant to him the loss of so many measures of rice and oil.

The crowd in the cage was getting thicker, and by sheer excess of weight the revolving cage refused to move. For, the booking clerk had fallen into a conversation with an old friend of his from his own village, whom he had not met for several years. His friend had now exercised the privilege of intimacy to call on him in his own sacred room and take the ticket from within, as a demonstration to the hostile and begging crowd before him of his special relationship with the lord of tickets. He went on talking leisurely of health, wealth and weather, making prolonged enquiries of sundry trifles at home. The booking clerk, sick of this damned work for ages with no chance of promotion, stopped his unceasing toil at the dating machine, stretched out his legs, and chattered at ease, yawning every minute the yawn of freedom.

Only five minutes more for the train to start, and the first bell rang. The sound was death-knell to the frightened sheep in the pen, and they redoubled their god-given bleating devices. But the lord of tickets chewed the *pan*, and rolled his tongue with the new-comer occasionally digging out a particle of nut that got in between the aged, decaying teeth, and shooting it out in sportive triumph.

Rangan had just arrived within the cage, and loudly protested, " What does the booking clerk do there, sleeping ? "

The booking clerk crashed, " Who are you, *dorai* ? When did you arrive straight from London ? What did you do till now ; these fifty-five minutes I have been issuing tickets—sleeping or wooing ? "

But Rangan's words had some effect though not immediately. For the clerk began to pull out tickets once again, and the familiar click of the dating machine carried joy to Rangan's palpitating heart and to the sweating crowd in the cage.

But with the sheer excess load of men the revolving cage refused to move, and no new-comer was willing to go out and ease the load. So one by one as soon he had secured a ticket, scaled the height and leapt out like a prisoner escaping to the freedom that lay beyond.

Rangan saw the prospect with dismay. Rajeswari was standing a little away, lost in international melancholy. Rangan's turn came in a couple of minutes of suffocation. He got the tickets, looked high and prayed to his family God, the Lord of the seven sacred hills at Tirupati, scaled the cage with trembling hands—muttered a curse on the railway administration and the British Raj, and leapt on to the ground with no greater injury than a twisted wrist, a crushed toe, and a neck that refused to revolve its usual swing of freedom.

"Dear Rajee, after this you won't plead for Swaraj. Such a thing as we have witnessed now is unthinkable anywhere else in the civilised world. Even after years of railway service, if we can't learn to fall in a line and form queues—we are unfit to take a single step in advance. Anyhow the booking clerk has been scandalously negligent—I shall report him to the Agent as soon as I go to Tanjore. I'm glad I have had this experience to-night though it's frightful."

Rajeswari interrupted, "Let us catch the train first—then there is plenty of time to philosophise in the third-class and to think of remedies."

A little away from the horrid cage, stood a constable in khaki shorts and red turban, listless and laughing, chewing gum, *pan* and tobacco, and spitting all over the marble pavement. Occasionally he varied his ease and stopped his chatter casting eyes on some fair passer-by. Rangan went up to the constable and complained.

"It is none of my business, sir, to form queues. This sort of thing goes on from day to day. Nobody thinks of it as anything unusual. Evidently you are new to this place. I've orders to catch only thieves and pick-pockets."

"The whole system is wrong, Rajeswari. No tinkering will cure the malady. There must be some strong purging. Some Mussolini or Napoleon, India needs at this critical hour: a man of action who will do things quietly and clear the debris of ages. These chronic tumours can't be cured by fasting, but must be cut open and cured by a surgical knife. Mild measures are no good, sheer waste of God-given time and energy at the most critical and fruitful hour in our history."

"Let us catch the train, Ranga, this is hardly the place for preaching or for political philosophy. Let us move on quickly; barely a minute. Let us discuss things in the train—if we are so lucky as to catch it for all this adventure."

Rangan hurried elbowing his way through the crowd, pushing aside a few, young and old, men and women, quietly forgetting his own Sermon on the Mount and his philosophy of queues.

Rajeswari Bai silently and quickly followed him, with her bag in her own hands, wrapped in thoughts of sadness at the fallen condition of her land of birth.

CHAPTER VI

THE BOAT MAIL

(1)

WHILE Rangan was thus performing rare feats of acrobatic skill within the protection cage in front of the booking-office window before the immediate presence of Rajeswari Bai, the Ceylon Boat Mail lay on the first platform like a queen in her bridal chamber awaiting her lord. The engine was fifty yards away from the coaches, 'drinking' water with a hippopotamus grunt of satisfaction puffing smoke and emitting occasional sparks of fire as if to tell the starlit sky above of a kindred power in its bosom.

The Ceylon Boat Mail is a thing of beauty, a favourite of the railway gods at Trichy. It is their darling and the one thing they care for among the thousand wheels and brakes that clatter along the two thousand miles of their railway. It had that day a special freshness and charm. For the first and second-class coaches had been newly built and painted on a new model of comfort and colour-effect for the ease and pleasure of those that travelled back to England after the weary work of years in a trying climate. And the third-class coaches also on such a festive occasion could not escape a touch of paint and varnish. The net result was that the Ceylon Boat Mail that day fascinated Rangan by its queenly air of freshness and seemed to him as if it had been specially made for Rajeswari's first South Indian tour. And Rangan, ever sensitive to all sensuous effects, would have praised the whole as the finest work of man and of British Raj in India but for the tragic story of third-class tickets to Tranquebar.

It happened to be a Rangoon steamer day. A deck cargo of two thousand men had alighted at the harbour that morning and some of them were speeding home if possible by the fastest train. So the Boat Mail carried double the human freight it was meant to carry. Every coach was a litter of boxes and beds, men, women and children huddled together in amusing postures.

(2)

It was only five minutes for the train to start. The Station Master, a stately figure who had done justice to all the good things of this earth, emerged, from his lordly seclusion and condescended to join the crowd on the platform. He cast a fleeting glance of contemptuous pity at the terrible, 'black-hole' congestion in the third-class coaches, and sniffed at the 'blackies' who all wanted to travel by the same train. The next, which left an hour later, he was sure, would go empty. It was impossible to deal with traffic congestion in South India with people of this mentality. Passengers go like sheep to the same compartment and the same train, and don't even bleat!

He strolled on the platform gracefully like a God among men, and there was a hushed discipline and decorum among the menial staff of the railway. He never spoke a word to anyone till he met the Chief Inspector of Railway Police and asked him, smiling and surprised, "I'm very glad to meet you, Inspector; you have become somewhat rare nowadays. Any important work that has brought you here in the midst of the crowd? Can I be of any use to you?"

"Yes, I'm under telephonic instruction from the Commissioner of Police himself to watch two persons travelling by this train."

The Station Master gracefully nodded and pursued his way towards the engine.

While Rangan was struggling in the cage to obtain a third-class ticket, a 'phone message was received at the Railway Police room of the Egmore Station.

"'Hullo, is it you, Inspector, I'm the Commissioner of Police, Madras City, speaking. Urgent orders have been received to watch the movements of Mr. R. S. Rangaswami, Assistant Collector, Guntur, now on transfer to Tanjore. He is leaving Madras by to-day's Boat Mail, with one Rajeswari Bai, a fresh arrival from Bombay this morning. A special C. I. D. is being sent immediately. Watch their movements and locate them in the train so that my man may easily spot them if he arrives there just at departure time.' "

The Chief Inspector had but six months to retire on his full pension. He had reached the summit of his ambition, and loved more the armchair in his office-room than the crowded platform with luggage scattered, over which he might trip and fall. But now that the Commissioner of Police had personally telephoned to him he leisurely began to make enquiries and at last succeeded in identifying the luggage-heaps in the first-class. He posted himself in front of it when he met the Station Master who, after the casual enquiry, steamed off to the engine-driver, curling artistically fine rolls of smoke from the cigar in his mouth.

The porters who handled the luggage of Rangan, they too were waiting for their wages. The police Inspector asked them in a commanding voice, " Where is your man, fellows? It can't be he is not coming, leaving in the train so much of luggage."

" No, no, master, we saw him with our very eyes —a lean, tall, lanky common sort of fellow. Please ask the ticket-collector. He'll tell you more."

" You must be wrong, idle fellows. He can't be the man—the Assistant Collector of Guntur. The fellow you describe must be his servant who is even now perhaps waiting outside for his master. But it is only three minutes for the train to start! "

He looked at the big clock uneasily, lest some random stroke of ill-luck in work like this, though outside his usual orbit, should mar the closing months of his even career.

Nobody came, but at the last moment a well-dressed young man ran up to the Chief Inspector hurriedly and whispered into his ears, " Thanks, it's all right. They are in the third class, secure. I've just put them in and found for them a seat, when they were knocking about. Only their luggage is here. It's strange—first-class tickets for one's luggage and third class for oneself! But there is plenty of time to solve the riddle in the train. Politics, ever a puzzling game! Good-bye, master. You don't remember me now at this distance of time, but I'm your Ponnan. I first entered service under you six years ago at Villupuram as Head Constable; now I'm much better off—in the C.I.D., thanks. Good-bye, for the present."

Ponnan gracefully saluted his whilom chief and darted off like a terrier that was sure of its scent.

The old man, the Inspector, was wondering at the cleverness of these spy-hounds, while he himself, an old head with the red turban on, soiled with the sweat and dust of thirty years, could not get even an inkling of it.

Before he could wake up from this admiring reverie and congratulate his old constable on his alertness and good luck, the Boat Mail gently whistled and moved on quickly and silently, like a dark cloud among the stars.

CHAPTER VII

THE ETERNAL FEMININE

(1)

THE beautiful, little railway station of Akkur, new model, stands in a shady grove on an arching curve of the track, like a bird on the leafy branch of a mango tree.

The soil is fertile. All around the vegetation is rank and luxuriant though so near the sea. The cocoanut trees peer into the sky. Giant banyan and stately mango cover the earth with a deep shade of solemn green. Life in Akkur seems a little idyll. The railway line gives it only a fresh charm, a snake-like beauty and fascination.

The little dots of pure white buildings in the railway compound look like huts in a hermitage. The station seems a place for reverie, and no wonder even the trains move so dreamily, whistling a love tune to the bracing winds from the sea.

The sky was almost free and the crescent Moon seemed to crawl and play with the wayward, floating shapes of thin cloud. A steady breeze from the sea was blowing in, and Akkur, standing on a little eminence of its own, received it to the full.

No. 10 had already left for Tranquebar leisurely winding her way to the lull of the evening sea.

(2)

The clock struck eight. Sundaram had practically finished his work for the day, and rose to go to his residential quarters near by, blithe as a bull to its feed after the day's hard work.

Sundaram was a *karmayogin* in his own humble way. He believed in work, honest, absorbed work as allotted to each according to his own inescapable *karma*. His juvenile days were no doubt of stormy truancy but he gained a varied experience from life and a quiet philosophy of work. He had therefore developed a tender affection for the flag, the key, and the telephone and even the railings that marked off the sacred station premises from the land of the common folk.

Hardly had Sundaram left the station yard when the purest strains of *veena* music filled the cool evening air with an ecstasy that Akkur had never known. The crescent Moon poured steadily her mellow light. Even Sundaram's ears accustomed to the rumbling of trains and the creaking of dilapidated old coaches felt charmed by the subtle ecstasies of *veena* in the vast silence of Akkur.

In a minute Sundaram stood enthralled before his own wife.

(3)

"With the *veena* by your side, you look indeed goddess Sarasvati. I know you won't feel lonely in lonely Akkur, though in Mayavaram Junction you felt very lonely indeed. What a godly change from the traffic roar of Mayavaram! Sarasu, Akkur is just the place for the ripening of your soul."

Sundaram knew very little of soul affairs. But he thought he must say something adequate to the occasion in praise of his cultured wife, whose perfect loveliness and flawless features he saw with ecstasy in his eyes. Sarasvati with the *veena* in her hands had a god-like grace and a serene look of *yoga* that comes after a perfect hour of absorption, self-realisation in music.

She looked at Sundaram with a strange lassitude as if her inner life had not yet returned to her body, and spoke in a low voice, "Yes, dear, this is the first full day I've known for many a year. Mayavaram Junction is not the place for music with its clatter of thousand wheels and the endless roll of coal-smoke."

"But, Sarasu, your music is so fine in this quiet place that I fear your *veena* will paralyse the motion of trains—nay, even draw the oldest of cobras from their hiding places."

"Dear, when you yourself grow so very warm in praise of music I too fear it may paralyse your No. 13, the next train that is due. But already one part of your prophecy has come true. The evening twilight was gracious and full and I was moved to the depths of my being with the raptured song celestial of Iyyarval's *keertanam*. The pot was simmering with milk on the oven yielding a rich fragrance. Our white cat, Seshi, slept to the music, forgetful of the rats that had already begun to move about and the cup of milk that was her due."

Sarasvati tuned the strings of the *veena* to some random rhythm as if to recapture a thought lost in the excess of emotion, and began again to pour her words in a voice calm and free as her own songs.

" In the height of ecstasy when music lived with the brooding silence and charmed the solitude, a long, long, shining cobra came winding along the verandha with raised head and spreading hood deeply fascinated by and lost in the music. The milk in the pot bubbled its own joy. The cat saw the shining cobra as if in a dream. But it moved not forgetting in the spell the ancient feud of the race. The dancing snake saw the milk and the cat and me but lost the instinct to strike and its native venom in the roll of music. I forgot myself in the soulful ecstasy of song and the serpent became only an added charm that churned me to the inmost depths of my being. I felt I was one with all, and felt for a moment the rapture of the great *advaitic* song: All Life is One. Such is the yoga of music: it gives the primal joy that makes you one with Nature."

Sarasvati's long and rich eyelashes stroked the eyes as if to refresh them from some age-long vigils. There was such a tranquil depth of life in her eyes.

"Dear Sarasu, will you sing once again that glorious song to me?" Sundaram asked her as if he were asking his family goddess for a favour. "Yes, I'll, dear, with pleasure. Perchance it may subtly change your view of life—that in these glorious days when a New India is in the making, you and I must do some nobler work for the country than letting in and letting out trains, something that would go to lift the downtrodden poor whom we see daily by every train crowding in hundreds, ill-fed, ill-clothed, ignorant and in misery."

Still the milk simmered in the pot giving the rich odour of slowly boiling milk. Sarasvati graciously took the *veena* that lay by her side and tuned the strings that seemed to wait for the raptured touch. The cat Seshi understood the delight, shrugged herself, lengthened out her tail, drew it in again circling it cosily round her bushy body, and lay ready in wait for the song celestial. Sundaram never in his life felt so much drawn to music as now, nor so intimate at home with his own wife as now. A day's life at Akkur had already worked a magic change.

Sarasvati was once again lost in the most perfect rendering of her favourite song. A yogic reverie was in the evening air. Time kept no count of itself.

(4)

Middle-statured, a little soft and plumpy, shining with the colour of burnished gold, Sarasvati looked a round-faced, perfect beauty. There was a virginal freshness in her face. The high brow, the rising forehead, the eagle nose and eyes, and the unfading lustre of a high-class Brahmin girl gave her a magnet charm, a marked look of distinction and aristocratic birth to which she had really no claim. Hers was a humble birth and her classic beauty was a strange gift of the gods in the infinite mutations of life.

Her father was an agent in the household of one of the leading aristocratic Mahratta Brahmin families of Tanjore. Though his pay was only ten *kalams* of paddy and five rupees a month, he was the real master of his master's household, and Sarasvati a darling to both. In such an environment of aristocratic ease, culture and refinement, Sarasvati grew till her tenth birth-day like the lotus in a sunny pool of water.

The great house had a sudden fall. It went into insolvency. For, the traditions of hospitality were royal without royal means, and three important law suits went against it in all the three courts from the Sub-court to the Privy Council. Sarasvati's father died with his chief, a broken-hearted man, when she was just ten. Her mother lived only to see her married at fourteen, and died as the result of an accident in the same year.

Sundaram was a remote, poor kinsman of hers. He was a bright boy at the College at the time of his wedding. But a strange ill-luck seized him almost immediately after. A wander-lust filled his mind once proficient in geography in the High School. He roamed all over India without a pie in his pocket as a young *sadhu*, thanks to the beneficent railway system which winks at a free ride of those who care to smear their bodies with the sacred ash, and tell the beads piously when the flying squad of ticket examiners click their punching machines emptily before them as so much of their own time and money wasted.

Somehow this roaming life for Sundaram came to an abrupt end when a kindly and young Assistant Traffic Superintendent, recently and directly recruited to the Service, discovered this bogus young *sadhu* at Madura. He sympathised with the story of Sundaram's wedded but truant and unfulfilled life, appointed him a ticket-collector at Mayavaram on promise that he would take in his partner and set up home and live a decent, settled life.

Sundaram's, as a ticket-collector and signaller, was a good record of earnest work. He fulfilled his promise and set up home. But even on the first day he saw that Sarasvati was too great for him, too much above him in every way; indeed, too great for the touch of man. He appeared to himself as a slender stream of struggling water springing from obscure depths, humbly flowing by the side of a mighty river which moved with all the majesty of a mountain-birth and inborn motion. He dared not break the lofty bunds of reserve and mix with the moving stream his humble tribute of love. He was content to live and move with her like a thread of water that oozes and struggles instinctively through mud and mire on the dry side of the banks of a flooded river.

But Mayavaram did Sundaram one definite good. It gave him back his old school-boy love of books. And one common trait cheered him, that Sarasvati too loved reading and became an absorbed reader of choice books, thanks to the local library and the Higginbothams' book-stall and to the friendly relations he kept up with its clerk, who shared with him the decent view that books are in the first place for being read, then for sale to those who buy but do not read.

Sundaram was tired of the strenuous work and night vigils at the Mayavaram Junction for over three years. When the branch line was opened from Mayavaram to Tranquebar he had his eye on Akkur, the coveted station on the line. He knew that Sarasvati would rejoice in the calm, the solitude and the grandeur of Akkur. And that she would play to perfect self-absorption on her exquisite *veena*. Yes, even on the first day Sarasvati with her *veena* kept spell-bound man and nature around her.

(5)

No. 10 on her return journey from Tranquebar was screaming at the outer as No. 13. Whistles shrieked with a revengeful noise and a petulant ire. Sundaram, the station-master, lost in the heaven-and-earth linking reverie of *veena* music, startled on hearing the whistle of a steam-engine and rushed out in bewilderment to receive the roaring train, crying at the top of his voice : " In the branch line, they have no sense of time. They come and go early and late as they choose. But that shall never be hereafter. Where is the scoundrel, Karian ? "

CHAPTER VIII

KARIAN'S VERSATILITY

(1)

WHILE Sundaram was thus absorbed in music Karian had an exciting hour after leaving the toddy-shop. Karian was a very popular fellow at Akkur, as he was the unchanging centre of attraction. Station-masters may come and go but Karians always remain like the solid rails on the railroad, and they are as imperative for the motion of trains. The work of a pointsman is varied and he is the one essential fellow who keeps up the continuity and gaiety of the ever-changing railway station life. Karian was the most vivacious of pointsmen who ever touched the points and side-tracked a train to the station yard.

Karian had his own free quarters within the beautiful and shady premises of the Akkur station. But it was so small a cubicle of solid brick and mortar with a little aperture for light and air as to make Karian think that it only enhanced the menial nature and the slave's mark of his job, to confine his roaming spirit and expose his household to the jesting looks of enquiry and the prying gaze of every passer-by in the train.

Though the rules did not permit it, Karian practically lived a furlong off the station in a little cocoanut garden of the village proper in an old-fashioned house. His wife came of a decent family still partially clinging to the ancient holding in spite of the disruptive influence of modern refinements and luxuries. This doubled his obligation not to expose her to the vulgar gaze of railway passengers.

But Karian himself was a gay fellow still young. He had seen much of life in his dashing younger days when he levied his pleasure from the fairest of the surrounding young. Many villages lay at the mercy of his predatory amours, and it was only the waning reputation of his family and his purse that curbed the scope for the legitimate expansion of his juvenile ideas of conquest.

But his wife led a very virtuous life, loyal to her lord, and brought up with care and love her four children, whom Karian viewed as the living symbols of weak and insipid moments in his most accomplished life of amatory adventures.

Karian was growing more irregular especially after Kandan's arrival as if to emphasise the diverse quality and richness of the same stock. And recently a young girl of fifteen, fair and fresh as a flower not yet plucked from the stem and knitted into a garland, charmed his attention. He spotted her one evening alighting at the station like a fairy from the blue sky. And he knew not a day of rest thereafter. Even the rumbling of trains grew faint to his ears which rang with the echoes of the silver peals of her merry and innocent voice.

Karian often exclaimed in reverie-talks to himself, "The little, blue bird, with so fine a plumage, still fluttering about hither and thither from branch to branch; not yet caged even for an hour. At the worst, I'd take her as my second wife." Karian had long ago decided on another and waited only for a suitable lady of youth and beauty. Even in his drunken hours Kamakshi was his sole thought.

Immediately after taking leave of Kandan so fraternally at the toddy-shop, Karian hurried home as best he could after so much drink to his credit. But his progress was arrested on the way by the unexpected vision of the beautiful Kamakshi who emerged on the main road from a by-path, and met Karian suddenly. She was carrying a bundle of plantain leaves neatly rolled-up and a bunch of fruits, a rattan box and a cosy, little bed. Evidently she was on her way to the railway station.

Was the bird taking flight all of a sudden, even before he could make one real attempt to catch her? Karian even in his drunkenness thought so far very clearly. For drink gives both drive and clarity to certain matters of the flesh. Kamakshi's bird-like beauty, innocent and unwedded, had a fascinating and pulling charm for Karian even as the full moon to the sea.

"Sweet girl, Kamakshi, where goest thou in this dark night all alone?"

Karian bravely seized the situation being a veteran in the art.

"To the station, Karia; to Mayavaram, a wingless, homeless little bird has but to go forward hopping from tree to tree. Is it not time for you to receive the train? You are still here?"

"There's plenty of time. Don't fear, I'll guide you—the night is dark; don't go alone. I'll buy a ticket for you, Kamakshi, and put you safely in the train: a full compartment reserved for you as if you were the collector's wife, a *doraisani*. Come home with me; I shall run up and take a morsel of food. Then we shall both go to the station."

The voice and eyes of Karian became significant with the look of violent love. Kamakshi, a shrewd girl aided by the instinct of protection native to her sex, smelling the drunkenness of the man hastily said, "I'm not a funk. I'll find my way to the station. You go home and get ready to do your duty. And it is time for you to be at the station. I may miss a train, Karia, but not you."

So saying, she moved hurriedly on with a decided gesture of alarm, lest he should try to molest her.

Karian was at least for a kiss in the inviting loneliness of the banyan tree and such a chance would never recur. Smart girls like Kamakshi never yield to mere cooing, sweet words or verbal entreaty, but always surely to prompt and sweeping action. That was Karian's triumphant and incisive way of looking at things feminine. But he heard the rumbling of wheels at a distance and a slender row of Dietz's lanterns glimmering between the avenue trees. Karian's better sense prevailed even in his drunkenness. He sped home considerably alarmed and agitated at his own ill-luck and lack of final courage, and with a doubled grievance against his own wife.

(2)

Karian had not brought home a pie of his earnings for over a month, not to speak of his extras for the week. With her own slender means from her father's, Karian's wife was keeping up bravely the show of her household. Too proud to borrow, for the first time in her life she thought of borrowing a measure of rice from her neighbour that evening. But she could not gain the courage to do it. So she waited, straining her eyes and ears awaiting her lord.

On hearing footsteps, she opened the door. But to her surprise it was not Karian but Kandan. She retired gracefully towards the kitchen.

"Madam, don't be afraid. Karian and I have become friends this evening, once again dear cousins. Has Karian not yet returned home? I thought he should have by this time. But that doesn't matter. How are matters with you *anni*—

children doing well? Why, I see no signs of light or even the kitchen-fire."

Meanwhile, the four children came crying to Kandan's knees and asked for sweetmeats and food. Kandan took in the whole situation at a glance and muttered to himself, "Karian has been drinking away the money! I see it all—here is a rupee *anni*, for the children. I should have brought with me some sweets. For, as the old proveb goes, never go empty-handed either to the temple or to children." Kandan tried to philosophise in a very homely manner, as best as he could catch the graces of home life.

Kandan flung a rupee gently to her. The silver piece cleared half the ground and clanged on the mud floor. The echo had hardly died when Karian burst into the room, in what mood, we know!

"Kanda, you are here—all alone, making love to my wife? Is it for this you befriended me this evening in your own wily way—and this silver rupee in the middle of the room—token of the bargain?" Karian was in an unbounded rage and believed in the force of direct words.

Kandan tried to appease him as best as he could. "Dear cousin, do not lose your temper or wits without knowing the whole story. Sure that you would be here before me, I came just to continue and carry home the reconciliation, and also pay my respects to *anni*. Don't make any foolish charge in haste."

Kandan paused in vain for a reply. He boldly decided to challenge Karian's way of living.

"I guessed everything, your cruel neglect of your own wife and children : you've never brought home a rupee these days, and all are starving. It's a rupee given as usual to the children for sweets as a token of affection from their uncle; don't you hear them crying piteously before your very eyes?" Kandan thought that Karian must now be appealed to very touchingly and continued, "If you resent the offer, I'll take back the rupee. Your children are my children, Karia. Who are there for me in this wide world except you and your boys?"

But Karian was raging beyond the reach of reason or of kind and sweet words. He pushed Kandan roughly back and fiercely scolded him out with the clenched fist pointed at him in a drunken fighting mood.

A drunkard needs a morsel of food at home quick on his return. Finding none, Karian took a spade shaft that lay idle near-by and sent it hurtling down his wife's head. She fell stunned to the ground and lay prostrate and motionless.

Meanwhile, Kandan slipped a little to the rear of the house and watched. Hearing the crash of a spade on a human head he shouted 'murder,' 'murder' at the top of his gentle voice, a voice ill-suited to such critical and violent occasions.

The whole village thronged to the scene.

Just then No. 13 screamed at the outer and the searchlight played steadily lighting the whole track as if with moonlight. Karian ran doubling to the station. For even in his drunkenness and strife, he remembered, for the grip of office is so vice-like on the human mind, that on the second line there lay an empty train and the points were perhaps set wrong.

CHAPTER IX

THE GLORY OF WORDS IN THE GLORY OF MOTION

(1)

WHILE Karian was thus making amatory advances to Kamakshi, and Sundaram was lost in the exquisiteness of *veena* music Rangan was trying his diplomatic best to negotiate with his fellow passengers a decent seat for Rajeswari Bai in the crowded third-class compartment of the Boat Mail.

But Rangan's graceful diplomatic negotiations came to nothing. For the passengers were in no mood to part easily with space so preciously won. And they were resting with an air of fatigue like a victorious army nestling in the midst of their plunder after a heavy siege on an impregnable fortress.

The third-class compartment itself seemed a delightful combination of a museum and a menagerie. All kinds of beds, boxes and bags were there in scattered heaps of confusion, from the crude rattan of rustic workmanship to the latest models in finished crocodile skin that incidentally revealed the range of affinity of the heart of its refined rich owner.

The passenger traffic was no less varied, ranging as it did from two stalwart *bairagees* with an uncombed beard of half a century's real standing to the finished products of modern culture, Rangan and Rajeswari; from an orthodox Brahmin telling his beads to a half-inebriated Indian *dorai* in hat and kakhi shorts, puffing his cigar and rolling the smoke contemptuously but ceremoniously straight into the dilated nose of the fasting Brahmin, who in his impotent rage could mutter only curses and mix them up with his expiatory *mantras*.

But all this exquisite variety was but even load to the steam-power that pulled majestically at thirty miles an hour.

At last, Rangan had succeeded in securing for Rajeswari Bai decent seating accommodation though elbowed on one side by a rustic in loin-cloth and on the other by a burly *bairagee* pilgrim with the usual appalling black shirts which carried the mud and the dirt of every degree of latitude from Rameshvar to Rishikesh.

But Rajeswari gazed on the scene of third-class poverty and variety with the innocent wonder of a child, and the easy tranquillity of a keen observer.

But Rangan could not secure for himself a seat for all his cleverness in speech and distinction in address. He had been all along standing pretending ease but twinkling his eyes pathetically in search of comradeship. His trousered legs, a little long and lanky for the occasion, were caught between the militant knee-caps of a virile Muhammadan who temporarily allowed this indignity of touch, having been dazed by the glory of Rajeswari's beauty. And Rangan was keenly aware of his perilous position.

So, feeling alarmed, Rangan began a few diplomatic questions to see if there would arise any early vacancy near him, though he knew it for pretty certain that the Boat Mail carried only long distance passengers and his own destination was probably the shortest. With a sigh of resignation, he made up his mind to forget his situation and the ill-luck of the hour by some brilliant and energetic conversation, a display of his own verbal powers of which he was so fond.

(2)

"Rajee, I made a fool of myself under your spell and courted all these hardships unnecessarily at the third-class booking-office in a real moment of confusion."

"Yes, by buying first-class tickets for luggage, and third-class for men! That's surely the way of the Heaven-born Service!"

"Yes, very foolish indeed as I see it all now, quite as well as you do. And anyone in my place, Rajee, would have done no better. We might have travelled third with first-class tickets but that did not somehow strike me then, in that wretched, crowded hour with porters yelling at your feet, only five minutes for the train to start and you imperiously bidding me!"

"That's the fault of Collectors travelling without their camp-clerks to prepare notes for their guidance for emergencies."

"Don't be cruel, Rajee, in your own inimitable way. When did you pick up this caustic humour—there seems to be a revolution up in the air in Bombay. Your cross attitude threw me entirely off the balance. I was in chaos when you refused to travel first, which I had arranged for after so much of hard work and bargaining. Even riotous crowds I've faced with calm, but I couldn't quell you at all this evening"

"Nor the porters' riot of co-operation!" Rajee spoke with a smile. Rangan attempted a faint smile in reply but failed. For he was already feeling his legs give way under the cramp of fatigue, after all the miracles they had performed that evening.

"But even this is an experience which both Collectors and Congress women should welcome and profit by. I'm not sorry at all. Are you well off there, Ranga, comfortable?"

Rajee saw Rangan wrestling with his feet vaguely on the wooden floor with distress signalled in his face.

"Yes, I'm better, Rajee."

Almost at once the big toe of Rangan sent an S.O.S. message to his protecting arms, now paralysed in the crowd. For his toe was heavily crushed in the capricious movements, ebb and flow of third-class traffic. A throb of pain flitted across Rangan's face. But he bore it bravely in that hour of public trial of his fame and name. He finally extricated himself from the vagaries of his Muhammadan neighbour, dexterously wheeling a little more to the left nearer to Rajee. And this seemed to Rangan a paradise of safety. And his tongue was at once released in the atmosphere of freedom.

"But I tell you, Rajee, this last hour has made me thoroughly sick of men and things in India, our boasted ancient land of urbanity and wisdom. I'm quite sad at heart for the sake of our own people. How little we have grown in the true habits that make civic life a pleasure the world over! Fifty years of railway travelling has taught us nothing! We've learnt nothing, we've forgotten nothing. We've not improved a jot. See, our carriage looks like a parcel van in which the passengers seem perched like so many thieves. Why not book these extra things and put them in the van?"

"And trust the guard with all your valuables!" growled the Muhammadan who mentally regretted that Rangan had escaped his educative knee-grip, "and travel with no peace of mind! You may as well thrust your crying little child into the van because it is very inconvenient to keep her here. What harm is there, hatted sir, in spending one sleepless night out of three hundred and sixty-four sleepy ones? Every fellow with a hat on thinks that he is a *dorai* travelling first-class."

Rajeswari did not care to continue to listen to this conversation but kept her eyes on another man in the same carriage. She spoke in a low voice, "You see there, Ranga, do you make out that half-awake man at the corner near the window?"

"Yes, it's he who showed us in!"

"Yes, it's he who shoved us in in time, Ranga."

"We must thank him for his kindness."

"Yes, thank him if you please, and draw him nearer. I think he is a spy, must be a spy. I'm sure,—he's set on me to watch my movements."

"Impossible!" cried Rangan.

"Quite possible, you yourself said this evening that I was being watched. I saw him in another dress in the morning, just in front of the guest-house, bathing and swimming in the Adyar river, frolicking gaily like fish in a royal pond—and then dry and clean, carolling in the by-paths of the cocoanut gardens hopping and singing like a bird, craning his neck at every bush, flower and tree,—only a well-fed C.I.D. can sing like that, the sweetest tunes of indolence at the most critical hour of our national life."

"And really so!" echoed Rangan in wonder and alarm fearing that he too might be watched.

"And by the way that he is now looking at us with screwed eyes gleaming alternately at you and me; I'm sure that you are identified even in the third-class and you are also being watched."

"I also being watched—impossible!"

"Quite possible,—highly probable. For men like you gifted with so level and balanced a mind are loved by neither the Government nor the people. In truth, I think that on this man's report hangs your fate—Assistant Collector at Tanjore with Sessions powers, or a mere Settlement Officer somewhere on the Palni Hills measuring piously hill-slopes and river-valleys."

There was an inspired cadence in Rajeswari's voice.

"Rajee, there is a mystic ring in your voice. But take it from me, Rajee, I'll never be that: a Settlement Officer, as a mark of degradation, in this patriotic hour! The third-class affair has already bitten into my mind; to tell you the truth, has embittered my soul,—yes, I think British Raj has gained half its unpopularity by its foolish and indifferent railway policy, and the sad neglect of the poor third-class travelling public who are heaped together no better than bags in a go-down."

Rangan spoke with genuine emotion, a rare thing even in the midst of his fine periods. And Rajeswari watched intently the crater of this volcano in action, which she had thought to be extinct long ago.

"Dear Rajee, be sure of my words. Sometimes trifles hurt us too deeply and tenderly, like coal-dust in the eyes. Then even the glory of motion seems wretched."

"I'm glad, at last, Ranga, something of the old spirit is up in you, kindling you to something noble and making once again a patriot of you. Yes, let us call that man, thank him first for his kindness to us, and then watch the drift of his speech, and try to understand the strange wonder in his eyes, that seems to mask and misinterpret everything about him."

"Yes, Rajee, we'll call him up and thank him."

"If he be a spy as we suspect him to be, he will certainly be glad to give up his present, nice place by the window, and share with us this crowded latrine corner—for the sake of the duty, the duty that gives him the easy bread."

"The tainted bread," crashed Rangan in a harsh voice.

A quick-change was coming over him and Rangan perspired profusely at the forehead. There was a tremor in his voice and a deep roll of flashing anger in his eyes.

The Boat Mail seemed to tremble on the track, quail on the lips of the shining rails. It sped at forty miles an hour for the sheer joy of the gradient, winding along the lake bund like a serpent in its racing hour of love.

(3)

" Tranquebar, Ranga, the name reminds me of our saintly Kandan. Yes, Kandan is colonial-born, but is not Tranquebar the birth place of his ancestors ? "

This sudden reference to Kandan overtook Rangan, and his already anguished soul felt a keen throb of pain. Rajee knew the effect Kandan's name would have on Rangan.

" There was always, Ranga, a tragic glory in Kandan's ways, and he seemed to me to walk on earth with a firm but alien step. Kandan's was a splendid sacrifice—he left you so abruptly in the I.C.S., probation period when a royal life like yours now was in his hands—who will sacrifice a princely career like that ? Do you hear from him ? "

Rangan made no answer, for his head was in a whirl and speeded quicker than the Boat Mail. And he did not fully follow Rajee's tribute to Kandan's sacrifice.

Indifferent to Rangan's silence, Rajeswari proceeded in a calm and measured voice.

" He wrote to me in lyric prose a pensive note of resigned love-lornness and resolve to dedicate his life to the uplift of his Mother Country. The whole letter was sweet and short, and I saw the vivid, magic face of Kandan, the broad forehead and the calm shining eyes lit with the steady light of the man slowly but surely gaining the conquest of his senses. He wrote to me that he was coming home to his Tamil land for social and political work, some little selfless deed for his fellowmen ; a squirrel's little service for bridging the sea as he put it. I thought he would call on me at Bombay on his way home. Perhaps he changed his mind or never came at all. Ranga, do you hear me or are you fast asleep ? Does the lullaby motion of the train make you sleep—no doubt you deserve a first-class berth for your feats at the third-class booking-office but, alas, who gets his deserts in this iron age ? "

" No, no, dear Rajee, you are again at it, the unlucky turn of things for me this evening. Kandan's name put me into a reverie of very many long-forgotten things. Yes, I now do think with you that we didn't do justice to Kandan's sweet character and great sacrifice. Yes, he deserves all that you say. Unlike us, unlike me at any rate, he is a man of deeds, deeds not on grooved lines making but deeper the ruts of social life, but on lines of pioneering choice of his own. Yes, Rajee, he is a rare soul and a blessing to the whole world like the pure monsoon cloud that rains everywhere for the impetuous joy of scattering plenty to all alike."

" I'm glad, Ranga, that Kandan's name warms you up and sets free the true Rangan in you as I've once known you to be. This generous spirit is the true index of a coming change over you, a change of heart that gives me a joy that is beyond your knowing."

Rangan felt a secret flood of glory sweeping through his veins. And Rajee's lotus-eyes, ever-broad and daring, lengthened a little more changing to a fawn-like beauty and meekness.

"Yes, Rajee, your approval pleases me beyond measure. I know something more of Kandan, all to his credit, that would please you most. Kandan comes of a very ancient aristocratic stock, the finest blue-blood in the District—but now the whole lot very, very poor. They throve well once as headmen of a big village near Tranquebar, under the Danish rule. The change of Government to the British has wrought all this change for Kandan's family. Yes, you are right, under the British Raj, the Indian village has suffered the most cruel blow. None but the Collector thrives in a District, like the blue-gum tree sucking for its own feed all the moisture around, even as in an Insolvency none but the Official Receiver thrives. It's the old, old story of the monkey that adjudicated the difficult, delicate claims of cats over a stolen bit of cheese."

"Many thanks for your roaming stories and rich parables. But what about Kandan? You know anything of his movements now?"

"Know nothing; that's why these figures of speech; and they are so easy and helpful to fill up the gaps."

"Kandan's father did some excellent work under Mahatmaji. Ranga, I think that thought of his father's work has set free the patriot's soul in Kandan."

"But I rather think, Rajee, that disappointed love of you,—remember, your appreciation of Kandan was not half so warm as it's now,—that unreturned love was thrown inward and changed to love of the great Mother, a thing, I think, so natural and lovely to all higher minds. And I'm pretty certain that if you reject me as well, surely I would court a patriot's death peacefully and nobly."

"I wish then at least for my country's cause that I might have the courage to make a patriot of you," Rajee spoke in halting tones somewhat unusual with her, and blushed a little.

"And yet there is something more, Ranga; the itch for service is in the blood. There's something in ancestry, something in pedigree. The headman of a village for generations can't help doing even under changed and poor conditions some public work; for the thing is in the blood."

Rangan rubbed his hands with impatience.

"It's but right, Ranga, that colonial-born Kandan should do something for the Mother Country at this most auspicious hour."

"Kandan is not colonial-born, Rajee, though it is true he is thoroughly colonial-bred. His father's flight is a most romantic story. Kandan's mother died while her little babe was but six months old.

Nallappan fled to Natal taking with him Kandan, then a little boy of three."

Rajee listened intently and cried, "Truly romantic and brave flight—all this adventure should have some hidden purpose—Nature's own mysterious ways. What a splendid sacrifice Kandan's life has been, Ranga! It's a pity I didn't know his true self at Oxford."

Rangan's mood suddenly changed, and he faltered almost in unconscious confusion.

"Ranga, why are you feeling confused suddenly? Is't that old thoughts are flooding you again and tormenting you now?"

Rajeswari flung a look of scrutiny, and began again with a voice that seemed to take its sound from the depths of her being. It had the ring of a serene decision arrived at after careful thought.

"No fear for my sake, Ranga. I'm no more the stormy petrel in the life of any one but my own. My marriage day is yet very far off. The love of my Motherland has driven off my mind all thoughts of love of worldly things. The call of my country has changed all thoughts of selfish life into deeds of service and the love of home has changed to a love of the whole world. A vow of *brahmacharya* has seized me till freedom's cause is won. That's why I think our ancients have consecrated the *sannyasin* order of men to work for the commonweal and the spiritual welfare of our race—transmuting the sex-energy into the purer and higher forms of work, work that is worship at the altar of universal life. God, in some great moment of grace, has whispered to me this secret, the secret that gives purity and strength to all acts, gentility and love—the healing touch of the gods."

These words uttered in a cadence of utter sincerity profoundly moved Rangan as it seemed to *illumine* for him some strange, hidden corners of life. But he knew at the same time that these words sounded the death-knell of his hopes and ideas. There was such a pure glow in Rajeswari's face and a ring of dedication in her voice that Rangan, the base metal, felt the alchemic touch.

The glory of motion at forty miles an hour quickened the glory of the winged words, the poetic fancies and intuitive flashes of Rajeswari.

Rangan simply tottered on his aching limbs, aching after an hour's most indecorous standing in the most public place. The crowded hour seemed to him more confused still, and the speeding train appeared to run the wrong way. He felt a thoroughly lost man in half an hour. But the mere sight of Rajee revived him and made life worth the labouring for, with all its strange turns and twists, turns and twists that sometime ago seemed only for your marring but now might prove to be to your own making in the long run.

"Look again, Ranga, that man is still at us, his eyes lengthening into a prying gaze from the window corner."

"It may be, Rajee,—you are not conscious of your own classic beauty—it may be that he is just vulgarly looking at you as so many fellows do when you pass by."

"But Ranga, I'm old enough, to class that one from the other—the prying look of the spy and the *vacant-dazed look of the lover—the lover* of fleeting beauty that escapes his hands like a shot of sunshine in a clouded day. Don't bring out idle theories, Ranga. It's not yet too late to thank him decently for his nice help at a critical moment, when your courageous leadership failed. You do it if you can, or confess you leave it to me." Rajeswari raised her whispering voice at the end almost to the heights of an impatient command.

Rangan, cut to the quick by the sharp and reprimanding voice of Rajeswari Bai, began to act with expedition.

(4)

Wheeling a little to the right on his legs, for still he was standing and the base of his operations was narrow, Rangan called out in an ingratiating voice, "Thank you very much, sir, for your great goodness to put us into the train at the last moment when we were running about for a seat. We are glad you are also travelling with us."

Ponnan made a gracious nod of acceptance of this belated thanksgiving and said, sitting still, and showing no desire to change place nearer to Rajee.

"Don't mention it, is it not our duty when first-class gentlemen like you choose to travel third for the mere sport of it?"

Rangan got alarmed at the extra knowledge he seemed to possess about them.

But Ponnan continued in a very even and undisturbed voice, "The third-class is generally overcrowded. Government should move in this matter promptly, and redress an ancient and real grievance of the long-suffering poor; then alone these—trifles to the ruling rich but great hardships to us—could easily be set right. And also the people's representatives, Council Members and Rao Bahadurs should give us the lead. But, alas, they travel always first-class at our expense! How could they feel for a thing they care to know nothing of?"

"That's the curse, sir, look at this," Rangan wailed, sloping his neck, "getting two third-class tickets has cost me this at Egmore, a sprain of the neck and the wrist. And we owe it to you that we got at all into the train." Rangan spoke loudly, craning aloft his neck like an uncrowned king.

"But, sir, when gentlemen like you with respectable ladies travel third for the mere fun of it, you should come at least half-an-hour earlier, and not at the nick of time."

Rangan wished to explain but there came a stroke of eyelids from Rajeswari, soft as lightning through clouds, conveying caution. And Rangan also felt that it would be too much to reveal the full tale to a stranger, though his righteous anger deserved all available outlets for expression. So he simply nodded apologetically and said: "At this rate, British Raj will come to an end—not so much by the Congress shouts but by this blighting neglect of the people in their truest need."

"True, sir," Ponnan eagerly intervened, "this neglect embitters the mind for a moment but leaves no scar behind or an open wound to bleed for ever—it is like the sparks that fly from the engine; these grievances die, the moment they are born. But there's another thing, a truer cause, the neglect of these poor fellows, voiceless and dumb, even to utter the deepest cries of pain; have you ever, sir, studied their lives in their villages, seen their abject misery at home,—wife and children not knowing where from the food would come for the morrow? Theirs is a cruel lot in this callous world; willing to work but no work anywhere. Even if they work the hardest, it hardly suffices them for the needs of the day, and the morning sun rises again as bleak and cold as ever. So lean and wretched lives you can see nowhere among God-created things, vegetable or animal life. Their cradle gift is chill poverty, and they are blessed all through life with nothing but grinding labour. Hungry hours crowd round the crying voice of children, and the maternal heart sobs in despair. These innocent cries of millions that go mounting up the skies to

Heaven will surely break the British Raj very soon."

Ponnan addressed this speech more to Rajeswari than to Rangan. And both listened to the patriotic and keen-sighted words with loving wonder. Rajeswari's compassionate soul was kindled to generous warmth at this stranger's love for the poor of the country. She cried out in a real burst of joy, "What's your name, sir? You are wise beyond your age. Your analysis is correct, so simply put, and beautiful!"

"For, I'm one of them, madam,—landless, crushed, down-trodden millions."

"Your name, please?"

"Ponnusami; friends and noblemen call me Ponnan. I come from the Tanjore District of a good stock, long ago settled on the land but now very poor. I ran away to Madras ten years ago as a boy and I've wasted the best part of my life in all the ways of a degraded, urban life. The call of the village has come to me, thanks to Mahatmaji,—I've bidden good-bye to Madras. Now I'm going to Tranquebar—"

"O, Tranquebar!" echoed Rangan and Rajeswari in one voice.

"Yes, to Tranquebar, never more to return to Madras."

"Sir, excuse me; did I not see you in the morning, swimming gaily like a watersnake in sun-set hour in the Adyar river, and singing under the banyan tree like a bird?"

"Were you there near-by, madam? I never took note of men or women this morning. I was in deep communion with my Maker. And Nature around me was so grand. I was lost in the glory of the river and the sky, the sea and the land. Adyar brought back to me my younger days in the sacred Cauvery, the mirth of the rolling river and swimming therein from morn to evening. I'm fond of water. I touched Adyar to bid her farewell for ever, and render my grateful thanks for the very many hours of peace it has given me these ten years. I'm at heart a village bird caught in an urban cage these wasted years—and on the day of my freedom and farewell, I sang a song to my heart's content under the cocoanut trees."

"You are now going to Tranquebar?"

"Yes, to Tranquebar. Mahatmaji's call has come to me as well, the lowest of the low. I'm going to my cousin who is the flower of my family. His is a life of sacrifice as great as that of any patriot. Believe me, he kicked up the career of a Collector so that he might work for his own land and people. He is doing rural reconstruction work and has just now on hand some temperance work near Tranquebar, I understand. I'm joining him."

"His name?" Rajeswari eagerly asked.

"Kandan," cried all the three in one voice.

"Yes, Kandan, madam, how do you know him? I've not till now seen him, my own cousin. But all alike say that he is the very flower of life, and I'm indeed proud of him as my cousin."

"Yes, Ponna, Kandan is indeed the very flower of life. We know him well. We were together at Oxford. Happy we are that he is working now in his own village, and we have met you. Please take us to him. We are also going to Tranquebar," Rajeswari spoke with warmth.

"You are also coming to Tranquebar! What a lucky day for me! Indeed a new life waits for me from to-morrow," Ponnan spoke seemingly moved by the tide of events.

Rajeswari really felt that her suspicions were ill-founded and unjust. All the three had not a wink of sleep but spent together the remaining hours filling the ears of Ponnan (C.I.D. on his way to a C.I.E.) with the intimate story of their lives, their future plans of political work, and their deepest thoughts for the country.

The glory of motion of the Ceylon Boat Mail gave a hectic glow to the patriotic confessions of Rajeswari and the halting and occasional but bitter and defiant words of Rangan. Rajeswari spoke with emotion and sincerity, and Rangan kept on nodding assent. Still they were nods that carried within themselves the silent change that sometimes comes over men and things, even members of the Indian Civil Service in spite of themselves.

The Boat Mail thundered along the track emitting vainglorious clouds of smoke and long-trailing columns of sparks, as if asking you to admire her matchless speed on narrow South Indian rails.

A stray particle of coal-dust flew into Rajeswari's lotus-eyes. Tear-drops, like pearls, rolled down her palmy cheeks. Rangan and Ponnan gazed in wonder at their pearl-like beauty. But Rajeswari paid the pearls gladly as the price of the glory of motion, and as a warning from God to stop the glory of words.

(5)

" Yes, Rajee, we are nearing the famous Coleroon, a branch of the Cauvery, an instance where the daughter is richer and riper than her own mother." Rangan could not contain himself at the approaching joy of his own district and the sight of the sacred rivers of his own native land, that fertilised the life of a people with a very proud culture and civilisation, "See yonder, Rajee, in the moonlit night the beauty of the infinite stretch of sand from bank to bank, a mile wide."

Rajee looked out of the window somewhat philosophically as a matter of courtesy and nodded a gracious assent.

"You should see the Coleroon in floods, Rajee," Rangan continued feeling a little encouraged by her unusual acquiescence in his eloquence. " It's truly a sight for the Gods to see the oceanic sweep of the turbid waters. Compared with the North Indian Rivers, ours are rather shallow; but what they lose in depth and majesty they gain in repose and charm. And in flood time they are lovely in their own gentle way. After all, Rajee, next to fair women, rivers are the most perfect born in this ill-assorted world."

Neither the Boat Mail nor Rajee seemed to care very much for Rangan's sincere flow of poetic words. Rajee drew with charming *neglige* to full cover the diaphanous surplus *saree* that rippled over her head with bird-like grace. The Boat Mail did not seem to slacken the speed out of deference to the great bridge as other trains seemed to do but simply thundered along the rails, the wheels shouting 'padak,' 'padak,' and drew up before the Coleroon Station in a whirlwind of dust to 'drink' water and rest awhile.

Padma travelling without a ticket could not afford the luxury of a stroll up and down the platform, leisurely selecting the least crowded compartment. So he quickly emerged from his hiding protected by the immense shadow-line of a giant banyan, and shot into the train to the nearest compartment. And it happened to be the very carriage in which Rangan and Rajee were seated.

"Rajee, this young boy seems to be the sole passenger traffic in this station." Rangan observed finding Rajee listless to his remark, "The next stop is Mayavaram and we must get ready."

"Get ready with what? As for your luggage, I hope it is safe in the first class, and really enjoyed the lonely run."

Padma with some effort could have secured seating accommodation but he dared not. So he kept on standing near a doorway-corner shyly rolling his eyes all about him. But he felt no fear. He seemed to have gained after the midnight bath in the Coleroon a fresh courage and faith in his own destiny.

Rangan, affecting keen observation spoke like a schoolmaster, "Rajee, this young boy is, I fear, a runaway from school."

"This being the examination time, naturally all boys who make good in life as patriots seize the chance to run away from school to do something in life, some good to the country."

"He looks so bright, Rajee, keen-eyed and lustrous. Just a boy like him would make for us an ideal personal assistant to help us in our plan of social reconstruction work."

"Then call him nearer, and offer him a seat, if a Collector cares to befriend a runaway school boy."

Rangan beckoned to Padma in very friendly gestures and Padma came affecting dignity to make up for lack of a ticket.

"Your name, my boy?"

"Padmanabhan, and my friends call me Padma."

"And Padma means?" Rajee turned to Rangan.

"Lotus," Padma replied and hastened to add, "in name, but in fact means only the mire from which it blooms for the glory of Gods."

"You talk wisely beyond your years, Padma." Rajee observed with loving interest fascinated by the courageous sweetness of the boy's voice and the clear, shining intelligence in his eyes. "Tell me, how far do you go?"

"On a long, long journey to Melbourne." Padma rejoined without a moment's hesitation.

"Melbourne!" Both Rangan and Rajee spoke in one voice of frank surprise.

"You know, my boy, where Melbourne is?" Rajee asked tenderly an innocent question in geography.

"Yes, it is in Australia, ten-thousand miles away; it is in a free country and that's my point."

"What for do you go on such a long journey?" Rangan asked still not believing his ears.

"What for? to breathe the air of a free country, to leave behind a slave nation of 350 millions—even if all were mosquitoes they will spread fever far and wide with every little bite—with all its ancient and incurable woes—freedom is what a youth longs for to gain so that he might grow to his fullest height, freedom from home, freedom from school, freedom from life—India is just the biggest pond for frogs, not for brave young men—our life is petty, small, mean and narrow everywhere. I may perhaps return ten years hence, like Lord

Reading, a Viceroy, or become a Mussolini with ample powers to work out a single glorious will and create order out of this chaos. To gain this rich will, sir, I must do *tapas* in a free, foreign land for ten years."

"You can do *tapas* even here, Padma, by self-less work. Five years of such good work will move on our social order to new and helpful lines. You can never improve a country by flying away from it, especially a young man." Rajee implored Padma.

And Rangan supplemented the entreaty in his own inimitable way. "Such work, my boy, will prune the dried twigs and branches in this ancient orchard till it begins to put on new sprouts and bear luscious fruits."

"It is all very nice as speech, sir, decorated speech. When you turn to real work, you find your work arrested, thwarted at every step by a whole array of vested interests and what not. The whole order must undergo a change in the same hour or there's no progress for a generation. I've some little experience as a public worker, though you may say I'm quite young and a mere school boy yet."

"You, a public worker! you are still a boy." Rangan was astonished.

"Yes, only a boy but don't you remember, sir, history, and that all good and great work has always been done only by boys, young but brave hearts and courageous, youthful hands."

"Then, let us know a little more of your public work at this tender age." Rangan asked with a half-cynical interest. But Rajee listened with real sympathy and Padma told fearlessly his favourite story of juvenile deeds and words.

Soon Padma, the boy-orator-patriot and Rangan, the Collector, fell into a very eager conversation. Rajee and Ponnan followed with deep interest the whole story of the boy's life till he actually got into their carriage. And Padma became as much a problem for the study of Rajee as Ponnan.

CHAPTER X

THE COLLISION

(1)

WE left No. 13 screaming at the outer of the Akkur railway station. Sundaram reached his office-room at one bound. The searchlight from the engine played steadily, lighting the whole track in one blaze of glory. While Sundaram was running in anger to lower the semaphore himself, he met Karian on the way who too came running with a look of equal promptitude and pained surprise.

Sundaram was in a rage. "You, jackal's son, where had you been sleeping all the while?"

"Jackal's son? May be, sir, but sleeping, surely 'no.' There was the usual trouble at home as there must always be between devoted husband and wife over meals not being ready. I beat her—that takes some time, you know,—one to get the other under control. Ere I could finish with her and get my food, No. 13 is roaring before time. Let her roar! These drunken, lazy loots of engine-drivers, black as coal and unsteady as sparks of fire from a flame, they must be taught a lesson at Akkur not to run trains before time." Karian was by nature endowed with a touch of fancy, and the toddy-shop and the exciting scenes of the last four hours made him a little more lively.

But Sundaram could not help asking even in such a crisis, " Beating your wife, Karia, to get food ! " But the train was screaming as if an impatient, juvenile, apprentice hand was at the throttle experimenting at the full range of steam-power.

" Karia, lower the semaphore, and see if the points are in order." For on the second line, there lay a ballast train with a few empty rakes.

Karian hurried reeling to the signal-box on the platform to lower the semaphore, and the station master cried out, "Karia, Karia, you seem to be dead drunk ; take care that you don't fall on the line and get crushed ; run ahead and see if the points are in proper order before you lower the hand."

"Who is dead drunk? Karian, no, impossible. The engine-driver is, I'm sure." Karian roared to himself at the top of his voice, "The points are damned always, always, all right in this petty station," and lowered the semaphore cursing and muttering to himself, "Come, come, you strumpet. I'll break your jaw even as I broke her head just now. Not a moment of peaceful home-life in this wretched work on the railways."

Hardly had the signal been lowered when No. 13 started thundering along the lines, after a long and shrill whistle that scared even the birds in the nests.

The key had been barely turned in the door-lock of the office-room. Sundaram had not yet reached even his coat and flag. There was a terrible crash as of engines fighting for way. The little vagabondish No. 13 ran against the ballast train which lay sleeping quietly on the second line.

Sundaram stood thunder-struck.

The crescent Moon was struggling through a heavy cloud.

Fortunately there was no injury to life except for a thorough shake at a chill hour. No. 13 came almost empty except for Chockalinga and his gay retinue. But Mr. Mudaliar did not travel as an ordinary passenger, but drove the engine with his mighty hand on the throttle and the driver by his side, presumably for emergencies. Chockalinga was naturally proud to guide a train himself on a track that was so much his own.

From enchanting *veena* music in the mellow evening hour with the crescent moon and the stars, and the open breeze from the sea, to the sudden crash of a collision, it was a startling transition even to such a well-balanced mind as Sarasvati's. She was indeed taken aback at the terrific sight of riding steel and smashed timber before her very eyes. Almost immediately, she was seen on the platform by the side of Sundaram, becalming the excited crowd and her husband by her tranquil looks and choice words of direction.

(2)

It was the first collision on the lovely virgin line from Mayavaram to Tranquebar. It was also the first collision for Sundaram as station-master. And for Sarasvati this strange and wild mating of steel and timber awakened a new impulse.

It seemed to her the sacred hour for the crashing of the shell and the bursting forth of a new and active life. It was a turning point in her life. The static became the dynamic and she felt a fine release of energy. The call of the country for work, for immediate work seemed to come to her in a flood. The flower began to feel within the stirring life of the fruit in the quickening joy of sunshine. The spring water from the bosom of the Mother has given up the sacred joy of secluded purity. It has risen to its full in the moonsoon hour of plenty to kiss the bunds and gain the freedom of the sloping valleys, to leap frolicking down the hills and glades.

And Chockalinga in equal wonderment was gazing at the moon-like beauty of Sarasvati in that dark hour.

Karian was more inclined to think of himself as an ordinary passenger than as the porter-pointsman of the station on whose punctuality and pluck of hand the safety of trains rests. At the first impulse, Karian thought of escaping like his great uncle to some foreign land, to avoid the perils of a prosecution. For he had heard vaguely that it was he who was in the first place responsible for everything that went wrong, from the screw that held firm the rails, to the mysterious engine that thundered along.

Kandan too was there at that unexpected hour. For he usually slept out in the open on the sand-dunes near by under a cluster of cocoanut trees by the side of a little stream. For sleep in the open air refreshed him after the patriotic fret and fever of the day. And he slept like a child to the music of the moving trains.

Kamakshi too was there frightened by the thought of Karian's amatory advances on the way, still perspiring with the sweat of terrified innocence and standing a little close to Sarasvati as if seeking her protection. But Chockalinga, the protector of all, towered high above the crowd.

Meanwhile, the whole village came crowding to the station to see the collision, a rare event.

Sundaram as soon as he recovered his presence of mind and powers of speech wondered at Mr. Mudaliar's presence in No. 13.

"Well, Mr. Mudaliar, how is it you are here by No. 13? You went out to Mayavaram by No. 9."

"Yes, but finding that my friend had left for Karaikal, I motored straight thither and spent an hour of delight with him—my Auburn, you know, races along with me on the roads even when I travel by train. Then I drove to Tranquebar and found No. 13 as I had expected, trusting to my good-luck in these matters, waiting for me, puffing and steaming."

"You drove the train?"

"Yes, just for a change from the monotonous, polished steering wheel of the Auburn car to the fiery grip of the throttle of a steam engine—what a warm experience—one can never forget this—but the driver was by my side. We covered five miles in five minutes;—oh, for the racing glory of speed, to drive an engine and enjoy its strokes of power and motion! But I never dreamt it would end in this. It is all Karian's work, his stupidity. I'll thrash him some day for this. I hope there won't be any trouble on this score, station master—only a bit of the old rust of the engine plates has been scraped off gratis. At any rate, Sundaram, I trust you can polish off the whole affair smoothly."

"I'll see to it, Mr. Mudaliar, don't worry your noble mind with these petty trifles that are parts of our daily lives. Where there are wheels, there collisions must be—Nature's law, isn't it?" Sundaram poured comfort philosophically into the aristocratic ears of Chockalinga.

With the born ease of a gay nobleman, Chockalinga pointed in return his fingers at the bags of silver rupees in netted purses that lay in mounds in the midst of his retinue.

Sundaram's eyes watered at the sight of the pieces of silver that shone through the eyes of the net.

"Don't worry yourself at all about this, Mr. Mudaliar; I'll see to it and set it right by to-morrow morning."

Already Sundaram felt as if he had taken charge of the money-bags, and felt inwardly the bubbling joy that comes of an easy, royal share in another man's riches. He turned triumphantly towards Sarasvati as if a new page had been turned to his credit in his career. But she was absorbed in another thought.

But Chockalinga was nodding graciously to all around him aglow with the fire of love, his tender flesh creeping and craving for expression. He was swimming in a dream of joy at the mere sight of Sarasvati's divine beauty, fortunately not above human reach, though there was a vague hint at the bottom of his mind of God's censure of his vile dreams.

Sarasvati, feeling the situation at a glance, reared herself, like a serpent in the hour of peril, to the full stature of her loveliness and womanly dignity. In that moment of proud feminine expression, she seemed more of the heaven and the starlit sky than a creature of earth living on rice, greens and pulses.

Sundaram slowly moved to his office-room, humbly beckoning Mr. Mudaliar. "It is becoming very chill here, Mr. Mudaliar, and you must be very much tired after all this jolt and travel,—and this strange end. Let us go and sit in the room—and you may even sleep on my office table. Meanwhile, I'll telephone to Mayavaram and set matters right. Karia, carry the bags of silver to the iron-safe."

Mr. Mudaliar accepted the invitation, for he was really feeling sleepy, in spite of the excitement of the collision and the kindling beauty of Sarasvati. Because all the five hours of the evening he had a crowded programme, and at Karaikal he had the best of it. Karaikal is famous for its cheap drinks, and Mr. Mudaliar raced all the way from Mayavaram to Karaikal at the top speed of his Auburn Sedan with a faint idea at the back of his mind that he might perhaps spend there a joyous hour or two, free from his responsibilities and cares in British India. He did spend indeed a couple of joyous full hours. For, his banker gave him five thousands instead of three he had asked for, and took from him a note for ten in the gay hour of revelry.

So Chockalinga was glad to spread himself out on the office table and there he soon began to snore. For, the young, innocent and aristocratic soul of Chockalinga could never sleep lightly. Sundaram, glad of it, bolted the door and rejoined Sarasvati who was still on the platform with Kamakshi. He soon cleared the station-yard of the miscellaneous surplus crowd, and prepared to think how best to wipe off the evil consequences of the collision.

CHAPTER XI

THE ARSON

(1)

SARASVATI under the starlit sky in the open of the station-yard, calm, graceful and lovely, waiting for the dawn like a lotus in the pond, seemed almost divine—more a witness from the stars to watch some strange tragic twist of life on earth. Her mere presence irradiated peace and strength of mind in that troubled hour.

The sand-dunes under the shade of a cluster of cocoanut trees, the little hermitage of Kandan, lay but a hundred yards off the station limits, by the side of a murmuring stream. But it was empty. For Kandan was on the station platform sharing with the excited crowd the sight of the collision.

" Who is the young man there looking so calm and noble in this hour of fright," Sarasvati broke the embarrassing silence in a clear voice of sweetness and strength, the twinkle of a renascent spirit beaming in her eyes.

" He is the first-cousin of Karian, Kandan by name. Though but a porter, Karian comes of a good family. Kandan's life is a romance, dear, more surprising than many tales you have read in fiction. He is colonial-born in Natal, educated at Balliol and living a life of love and sacrifice in the Tamil land!"

"Educated at Balliol, Oxford!"

"Yes, passed the I. C. S., only to give it up at the probation period. He felt the call of the Motherland as you too so often say you feel, reading the newspapers and the speeches of our leaders—he came over here but a year ago, and is doing his best to wash the dog into a horse, which no amount of washing could do."

"But it would at least keep the dog clean."

"Only the dog would go back again to the rubbish-heap to lie down upon curling its tail."

"May be, but still that work is noble. Look at Kandan, dear, there's real nobility shining in his face. That's a true worker with the virtuous glow of sincere, selfless work." Sarasvati began to read character from face.

"Now he is labouring for the uplift of the poor village-folk, spending money like water. He wants to do away with the toddy-shop at Akkur; for the last one month he is at it single-handed, picketing and preaching the virtues of a sober life to a crowd of chronic drunkards."

Sundaram cleared his throat and continued in a serious voice: "And our Mudaliar who is now snoring there in the booking-office wants to cut him down for ever. He says he is a rebel who disturbs the peace and the social order of his ancient kingdom —you remember he is the lord of two thousand acres. Dear, in a week, history will be made in our Taluk, and Kandan clapped in jail, perhaps, alas! Our Mudaliar has seen the Deputy Collector this evening and these money-bags give a rare executive power to Mr. Mudaliar's words. Nothing like the soulforce of money in these hard days!"

Mr. Mudaliar snored heavily in the office-room and through the key-hole came the nasal sound, rumbling as if a heavy goods train were moving up a steep gradient. Sundaram listened to this innocent surplus rhythm of sleep for a moment as if it were music, coming as it did from the nostrils of a rich man, the lord ot three hundred *velis*.

In Sarasvati's eyes Kandan was already a hero and a patriot and a martyr to the national cause so dear to her heart. She said, "Dear, you know him?"

"Yes, I know him a little. He came to me this morning to receive a parcel of *Khaddar* clothes and a dozen *charkas*, latest models, to distribute them to the poor. He thinks he can make men of these ignorant, drunken, lazy loots; petty thieves and rascals, the serfs and tenants of Mr. Mudaliar, sunk deep in the slime of ages."

"Still, dear," Sarasvati pleaded, "a beginning must be made and some one try his hand at rural work, the salvaging of these wrecks. I think it's the noblest work of our age to give a plan and an aim to these poor rustic lives and improve their lot. Why not we both join him in his work, and end this prisoner's life in this arid place—and my *veena* music will flow the sweeter and truer for the touch of selfless work. Sarasvati's bosom swelled with the deep earnestness of patriotic emotion."

Sundaram approached Kandan smiling welcome as the lord of the station. "Station-master," Kandan spoke with unaffected sympathy, "this must be a terrible experience for you. Whose mistake is this, Karian's or Mudaliar's? I fear you too will have to share in the consequences. If I can be of any help to you, I'm at your service."

"Thank you very much, Kandan. As there is no loss of life, I hope to polish off the whole affair easily with Mr. Mudaliar's influence and your good wishes."

Sundaram had hardly finished, when Sarasvati spoke in a quiet voice of self-introduction. "Rather, we would place ourselves at your disposal, sir, and strive to do some little work, the squirrels' best, in the country's cause."

Kandan's heart gratefully pulsed with delight at the silver voice and divine calm of Sarasvati's voice.

"We have heard of your work, sir, and of your noble life of sacrifice," Sarasvati continued. "Allow us to help you in our own humble way. This is the time for work in our country! When the wind blows, we must glean the grain, as the proverb goes. Two things we should work for locally: the toddy-shop must go, and Mr. Mudaliar must change from the oppresser to the protector of the poor. And we are sure to win under your leadership. Pray, accept us." Kandan nodded assent gracefully but could not believe his own ears.

"The curses of the sweated poor," Sarasvati paused a moment and began, "are now smouldering like a low fire on the heath and will break out into a conflagration at the first breath of the wind. Then granaries and hay-ricks as high as hillocks will turn to a handful of ashes ere this night breaks into day.

Sarasvati spoke calmly but a prophetic fire vibrated in her voice and lit her face with an uncanny beauty.

There was a sacred stillness in the air. Kandan stood raptured by the divine voice. Her cheeks, red as the petals of the lotus, reddened a little more. Her face shone with one tremulous patriotic glow.

Kandan was in a dream. Her nod of approval seemed to him the best reward for all his life work, the crowning bliss that saves even a man in despair and gives him renewed strength for work for another term of years.

(2)

Sarasvati turned a little aside to the east to cover the excess of emotion that surged through her. And she fancied she saw a beautiful glow of reddish dawn on the horizon. She murmured to herself, " It can't be the dawn. It is but eleven o'clock night."

But the truth dawned on her mind abruptly, and she almost lost control and cried out, " Turn a little to the east, Kanda. See yonder what this rising redness in the sky means? Are my eyes tricking me?"

Sundaram, Sarasvati, and Kandan gazed on in unutterable wonder at the increasing redness. Thin rolls of smoke came floating up with sparks of fire. That set all doubts at rest.

Kandan almost fainted and cried :

" Alas, Nandan, Mookkan, and Katteri; Irullan, Karuppan, and Irullappan; alas, Nalla, you too have joined them and have brought this ruin on me. Arson, arson, alas! the granaries and hay-ricks on fire; my fair name and work lost for ever! Nalla, you have ruined my year's work by a rash act in a drunken moment."

" Not only there, look hither, the toddy-shop too is on fire." Sarasvati's keen eyes observed another smaller roll of smoke in the neighbourhood and she pointed it out.

" I'll be held responsible for all this. It may be too late. Still I'll run up and see, and do my duty. Mr. Station-master, please stir the sleeping Mudaliar and tell him of his tragic fate for the night." So lamenting, Kandan shot out of the station like a man stabbed in the back. But

Mr. Mudaliar still continued to snore in the office-room.

"Twenty thousand *kalams* of paddy, worth half a lakh, and twenty hay-ricks high as hillocks—all burnt down. Mr. Mudaliar is a man ruined for life, and he won't recover at all hereafter." Sundaram uttered to himself these wise and calculating words of future estimate as he slowly regained his powers of speech.

In half-an-hour, the Akkur railway station became a regular pandemonium. Everyone came crowding to the station, as it stood on a little eminence of sand-dunes. From there, one could see with safety the progress of the fire in all its stages,—first the thin stray smoke resembling kitchen fire, then heaving, rolling and gathering into banks, wheeling high in the sky, mingled with sparks of fire, and finally the long, long, leaping tongues of flame.

There is a touch of the sublime in things on fire. It is a sight of fascinating terror to all alike. The rich and the poor, the safe and the imperilled, join in the wail, crying out for help, but admiring inwardly the speeding of perishable matter to the eternal home of the unchanging spirit. The wind that wafts the echoing cries of 'help,' 'help' from the admiring crowd of spectators does but fan the flames.

(3)

Sundaram was lost in wonder and thought. But it was interrupted by a telephone-call from the headquarters. "The new Assistant Collector of Tanjore is expected by the Boat Mail from Madras and stays a week at Tranquebar. Please get ready his morning-coffee at Akkur, just at the break of dawn. The local Deputy-Collector accompanies him.

"What about the collision—I phoned to you an hour ago."

"What about it! You'll be fired after the enquiry. You may now carry on for a few days. Railway dogs shouldn't be afraid of getting lame or being killed some day."

Sundaram's heart seemed to move up to his throat. But he beat the poor pulsing thing down with a determined will. Turning a little to the other side, he saw Mr. Mudaliar still sleeping and snoring like a big child; only the rhythm had a subdued cadence that comes of a long and earnest practice. His house was on fire but he dreamt of sparkling wine and lovely lassies.

Sundaram stirred him up, gently patting and prodding him at the feet with his red flag rolled up on its rod.

CHAPTER XII

THE LOOT

(1)

THE garden-house of Chockalinga was the ancestral home of eleven generations of territorial magnates who had originally settled there as minor military chieftains, charged with the guardianship of the marches of Coleroon under the Nayak kings of Tanjore. Chockalinga's family had a singularly rare reputation for an unbroken line of prosperity, till darling Chockalinga himself arrived on the scene as an infant prodigy, and began to squander the wealth and tradition of ages under the spell of youth and modern civilised life with its philosophy of a high standard of living.

The secret of this prosperity lay in the rigid exclusiveness and indifference to public work and welfare on the part of Chockalinga's ancestors, which resulted in an intense devotion to their own farm. And at last Chockalinga's absorbing interest in elections represented but the terrible reaction to generations of single-minded worship of self-interest.

And after all, this even prosperity of eleven generations is so repugnant to the sweet and native caprices of Goddess Lakshmi who delights to revolve like a wheel, the spokes of fortune ever descending and ascending.

(2)

The news of the collision at the Akkur railway station reached with the swiftness of a cyclone the ears of Chockalinga's aged mother while she was just about to retire to bed.

"Ramalinga, pray, run up to the station and see what has happened, for dear Chockalinga's sake; you don't seem to have even the idle curiosity of the common folk."

Ramalingam was her own brother.

"No fear, Porkodi, Chockalinga is safe. It's the Tranquebar train that has smashed itself against a ballast. Our boy has gone to Mayavaram and he will be here in half-an-hour in his stately Auburn Sedan."

"Collision! Ramalinga, it must be a dreadful thing! That is why I asked my boy never to work for these railway lines or metalled roads to our peaceful, pretty village homes. Our bulls are lying idle, like wild elephants, without work while the motor cars and the trains waste our hard-earned wealth. Pray, Ramalinga, run up to the station and see if my boy is safe."

"No fear, sister, he is quite safe and sound as a temple bell; he will be here in half-an-hour." Ramalinga opened his mouth wide in a splendid yawn that pleaded for comfort in the midnight hour.

"Ramalinga, why don't you tell my boy not to keep late hours like this every day and roam about doing other men's jobs and other people's elections for the empty name and fame of it. Our *pannai* is neglected; even vegetables and pulses we have now to buy from the bazaar—shame indeed! It would have brought tears to his father's eyes if he were alive to-day to see in his own son's days one hundred *velis* still lying uncultivated. This year at least Chockan must be married and made to settle down to the peace and comfort of home life."

"Yes, Porkodi, you have spoken wisely like a true mother. Marry him to a proper girl, and everything will get settled of its own accord."

Ramalinga warmly approved of the idea. For he had a daughter of marriageable age, and his one dream in life for several long, lean years had been to get her married to his own nephew, Chockalinga. That was why he had been watching and plotting and hovering around with infinite patience for over a year in his sister's house.

"Ramalinga, our *pannai*, the model for the Tamil land in Chockan's father's days is now a by-word of reproach to every passer-by. The *pannials* are crying for wages for the last three weeks and more

—these poor fellows, how could they work hard in fields in sunshine and storm, day and night, if they are not well-fed? Chockan's father fed them well, and every festive day in our home was a festive day for them as well. Our granaries were then full of all grains and pulses, and plantains and pumpkins rolled everywhere, and cocoanuts were mounded high as hillocks. Now the toddy-shop has come and ruined everything, and you can't get even one cocoanut to break before God Ganesha."

"That's so, Porkodi, the toddy-shop has weaned from work and thrift all our best men." Ramalinga nodded approval. For he was nearing sixty and still clung in common with his generation to some of the ancient Hindu ideas of piety and *dharma*.

"Ramalinga, in my days I have never known a single lean year even when famine raged all around. Chockan does not care for his mother's words, petted child that he has been. He has surely some respect for you. Why don't you tell him that he must soon mend his ways or our ancient *pannai* would share the fate of our cousin's at Sembarambakkam."

"Tell him these words only to lose the little respect I have still with him! Your Nallan, the *maniam*, is his chief minister; these things, Porkodi, are never learnt except in the hard and bitter school of experience. Wed him to a proper girl, and your future as well as his is quite safe, and see how he and our *pannai* thrive. It all depends on the girl you pick for him."

"The girl I pick for him! What are you going to do, Ramalinga? Are you going to Benares at the time of your nephew's wedding? You must select the girl for him." Porkodi paused a moment as if stifled by a transient thought, and then quietly added, "Why, I sometimes think that our *kutti* Neela, your daughter, will prove the right sort of a homely girl for my boy—only she is too young and not well grown-up."

"Not well grown up, our Neela! At the proper age she will shoot up like a plantain cluster after the first freshes in the river: that was the way with her mother. No, no, sister, at the bottom of your heart you think we are all too poor a lot. And true it's. But Porkodi, God has sent already a husband for every girl in our Tamil land." Ramalingam played the game very astutely and put up a very injured, shy, and sensitive face.

"No, no, Ramalinga, don't take offence at nothing. None is dearer to me than my own Neela. But you must play the game boldly and bring Chockan round. You know this half education and the spirit of the times have given him some faery notions about marriage. This twist of mind you should untwist, Ramalinga; you must pull him up and bring him round. If that be God's will, I'll welcome Neela home as my daughter-in-law next month." Porkodi spoke with warmth and decision.

"Yes, dear sister, Chockan is a fine boy; he won't go against your words in this vital affair though he may talk many strange things. Youth has ever been like that: always strange, dreamy, and eccentric in words but truly docile when the fateful hour comes. Matrimony will correct him and bring him to the true moorings of our family. Let him dash hither and thither a little and learn things for himself. That would teach him a lesson which he could really learn nowhere else."

"But, Ramalinga, he may be sucked in deeper and deeper into the whirling eddies of bad urban life, and everything lost like our cousin's at Sembarambakkam—and at any time it may become too late to recapture a lost young mind." Porkodi spoke with the anxiety and the pulsing breath of a mother, and Ramalingam like one cleverly fishing in troubled waters, like one manœuvring for a personal gain. For he felt at the bottom of his heart that Porkodi would not really care for an alliance with him if it were all fair weather before her.

"You are joking, sister, and Sembarambakkam is no parallel; for their lands are poor and the folk without prestige. But to waste three hundred *velis* at Akkur—it's impossible. Our *pannai* will stand half-a-dozen Chockans for six generations, no fear. Only this you must tell him firmly: that he should listen to my words a little more and give me some power to check and rule these unruly men in your *pannai*."

"Should he give you power, Ramalinga? As my brother you have yourself the right to it. Tell me who dares to contradict you!"

"Well, then, if you think so I shall deal from now very differently and teach a lesson to Nallan and Amavasai, the granary-rats. They are the chief cause for the fall of our ancient *pannai* these three years and more, and Chockan listens to their sneaky and vile words of advice."

"Ramalinga, I tell you now, dear Chockan has wasted in elections three lakhs in three years; take everything into your own hands; I should like to see my boy settled in life ere yet another month rolls by. This old body can't last for ever, and before I close my eyes in mortal sleep I must see Chockan married."

For the last twenty days two owls had been screeching at nights from the lofty ruins of the pagoda of a neglected Siva temple near-by, and its ominous shrill always carried terror to Porkodi's heart. The owls screeched again and wound up the auspicious words of Porkodi. She shuddered at the thought of some dire calamity to her ancient house. There was a death-like silence for a moment. But Ramalingam was busy planning his own future and his daughter's.

Porkodi broke the tense silence and cried, "The screeching owls forbode some dire evil. Pray run up to the station, Ramalinga, and see my boy with your own eyes; or I'll go myself. The collision is a strange calamity in our land."

Before Ramalingam could give her a comforting answer there was a terrible uproar of shouts and cries in the beautiful walled-in quadrangle, wherein lay like giants in sleep twenty grain-heaps and hay-ricks high as hillocks.

(3)

"Who are the scoundrels there, raising this uproar at dead of night? Where is Nallan, the granary-rat? Still at the toddy-shop? And Amavasai, the *talayari*—to give these thieving, howling loots some fine thrashing."

Ramalingam roared, glad to avail himself of the chance that came so early to exercise his new-born power in Chockalinga's *pannai*. And he turned round to his sister with the air of a wise and experienced administrator, and remarked, "Nothing good will come to our *pannai* till one or two old bandicoots are sticked to death—Nallan, the pious thief and Amavasai, the traitor *talayari*. Sister, I'll teach them soon a lesson with the lash."

But Porkodi was more absorbed in her own fears and in thoughts of her son's safety, especially after the ominous screech of the owls. The uproar increased in the granary and a thought flashed across her mind. She remembered vividly the audacious loot carried by her husband many years ago on a neighbouring village in which Nandan, Mookkan, and Katteri earned their pensions. And every year Porkodi expected the loot in return.

" Ramalinga, the owl has not been screeching in vain these twenty nights. I feared some such calamity as this to our house. I think these are the dare-devils of Sorakkai Thevan, out to loot our granary and our farm this night when my dear Chockan is away. Be quick, gather together all our brave fellows. Thank God that still Nandan, Mookkan, and Katteri are alive to teach these fellows the very lesson which they have taken fifty years to forget. Roll up your bed, Ramalinga, be quick; slip through the back door and call up all our *pallees* and *padayachees* and our valiant pariahs,—Nandan, Mookkan, and Katteri; Irullan, Karuppan, and Irullappan—the mere mention of their names, their footsteps will drive these fellows ten miles off. And Nallan and Amavasai are sure to be here somewhere near."

Porkodi was all action. She showed wonderful energy and agility at the ripe old age of seventy-two. Her commanding voice poured courage into the chicken heart of Ramalinga. Her tall and lean body still shone with the health and vigour of a pure life, like a streak of lightning in a clash of thunder, and amply justified her name, " Porkodi ".

But Porkodi's fears of a foreign raid were set at rest.

For, fortunately Nallan and Amavasai bellowed reverentially at the top of their voices, humbly standing at the entrance to the granary, and thus saved Ramalingam an awkward run by the back-door with a palpitating heart to the *paracheri*.

"It's we, ah, mother, your humble and devoted Nallan and Amavasai,—all our men are here, five hundred strong, crying for wages ; they are starving for the last twenty-one days. Pray, mother, master is away ; order our wages from the grain-heaps here. They have passed beyond my check or control."

"Wages ! scoundrels, at dead of night !" Ramalinga squeaked in anger at the top of his trembling and cracked voice. "No, no, you have come to loot, thinking us all asleep. I'll teach you such a lesson to-day that you'll never forget. Amavasai, you rogue, you are at the bottom of the whole mischief. I'll thrash you for it. And Nallan, you too are not doing your duty properly. A *talayari* and a *maniam* demanding wages at dead of night ; I've not heard of it anywhere all my life ! If only Chockan were here all would be flayed alive ! I must teach you a lesson, now or never."

Ramalingam took a long lash in hand and ran in a rage of frenzy to thrash Amavasai who stood motionless, like a Greek God, in the infinite beauty of his bare brawn and muscle. Ramalingam raised the lash for a stroke on his back. But Karuppan who stood near-by, like a ghost, caught it finely just at the stroking time and pulled the aggressor to a straight fall at his feet. Ramalingam's head struck the stump of a cocoanut tree and he lay senseless there for a moment.

Porkodi roared in anger raising her silver voice to the summit of old, old authority at this unheard of indignity to her ancient house. But her voice was not heard in the raging tumult, and her own household servants were thunder-struck and paralysed. The owls hooted again ominously.

Katteri, the veteran hand at a hundred loots till now in all places except his own master's, discovered at last that the dividing line to display the skill and courage of his hands was very thin indeed, and that the loyalty to the father did not and need not extend to the careless and undeserving son, especially when the pension had been in arrears for three months and more.

Katteri raised his voice to the clap of thunder and issued the marching orders for the night. "*Anné*, this is the richest hour for the poor *pariah*—it comes all too rarely, only once, half-an-hour in a long cycle of sixty years. These grain-heaps are the heaps gathered and mounded by our own hands. Our wives and children are starving at home these three weeks, and our master is away. Let each carry home as much paddy as he needs."

Nandan and Mookkan cried, "Hurrah, young men, go by our leader and carry out his orders. Long live our tribal gods for this hour of plenty! Long live our Katteri!"

The authority to loot was passed in the sacred voice of their own leaders. That was as good as God's own command to these loyal, simple tillers of the soil.

Irullan, Karuppan, and Irullappan, the most reckless and courageous of the younger leaders, shouted: "Set fire to the hay-ricks. The way is dark; let us have some light in this midnight hour. Let the voice of the poor go raging up to Heaven in flames, burning the sin and injustice of ages, and bring down the thunder-bolt of Indra on the head of this *pannai*. Our wives and children are starving while our master is making merry elsewhere, feasting in a royal way all the little urban hirelings, and underlings in official belts."

The voices united in the chorus-cry of plunder were grim and terrible and seemed to emit the pent-up fire and hate of ages.

An agrarian mob, unleashed by hunger in the throbbing hour of riot and loot, rages, leaps, and dances like a vast hill-lake that has broken its ancient bunds in the unlimited monsoon hour.

Nallan saw with dismay the turn things were taking under his overruled leadership. He cried with all the authority of the *maniam*: "Do anything you choose, fellows, in this fateful hour of madness, but don't set fire to the hay-ricks, the food of the dumb cattle. Loot the grain-heaps, if you please, and carry home, as Katteri says, as much as you can but don't listen to Irullan; don't touch a bundle of straw." But his cry and warning voice came too late.

For already a crackling, slender, shining fuse of fire was girdling, like summer lightning, round the black bosom of a hay-rick standing high as an elephant. Soon fire was everywhere raging, till it raised high winds as in a cyclone.

And Ramalingam was eye-witness to all this tragic scène in his own house, though he was not allowed a vertical view of the splendour. For he was held tight to the ground by the powerful hands of Karuppan who owed him some old grudge and kept on muttering: "You too have come here only to eat the salt of our master. Then why all this command and bluff?"

The *pannai* employed the labour of five hundred families, and, all told, women and children, it came to two thousand stomachs depending for their sustenance on Chockalinga's capricious moods. In this dark hour lit by the lurid, strange light of burning grain-heaps and hay-ricks, two thousand hands, young and old, male and female, worked at the terrible thing called plunder and loot. Everyone put forth the giant strength of hungry ghosts. All the grain-heaps and hay-ricks disappeared in half-an-hour, half by loot and half by fire.

Nallan wistfully gazed in impotent rage when a thought flashed across his mind and he cried: "Why, the toddy-shop the cause of all this woe alone escape. Pavadai, hasten to the toddy-shop, our curse, and the cause of my master's fall. Let a new life spring from these ashes."

Pavadai ran with a band of youngsters and set fire to the toddy-shop. And a sister light soon shone meekly but clearly at a distance. It twinkled like the celestial rays from the stars.

Kandan came running breathless but, alas, quite too late. He ran like a wounded hare, round and round the raging grain-heaps and hay-ricks. And Nallan prostrated before him and asked for forgiveness. "Great Kanda, this is not the work of man, but the act of God—a breath of wind and a spark of fire from the heavens. We had no thought of fire or plunder; we came only to plead for wages, long in arrears. But somehow it has ended like this in the twinkling second of a lightning thought. We don't know—who, how, or why. It seems to be God's will, and difficult times are ahead of us."

Kandan stood motionless, speechless, gazing in bewilderment at the two thousand looting hands, young and old, crowding, hurrying, and carrying home with throbbing hearts grains plundered amidst raging flames. The scene was too tragic for him to stay longer and he retraced his steps slowly to the Akkur railway station, Nallan slowly following him for some distance. Kandan knew at once that there were terrible things ahead for him to face.

But the loot continued in all the infinite fury of the hunger of ages, and the chance that comes all too rarely once a generation to the oppressed under-dogs of this world. This down-trodden race of pure tillers of the soil, with their feet ever in the mire of ignorance and poverty and their hands dull and palsied with over-work, are weak and listless like the sleeping tiger in day-time but are the most fierce and courageous in the dark and ghostly hour of loot.

Amavasai and Nallan, driven between two deep loyalties, stood like a ship caught in a tempest between two eddies.

But Nandan, Mookkan, and Katteri; Irullan, Karuppan, and Irullappan were gay and busy giving orders to their men, singing to the glory of Fire the purest songs of pleasure.

CHAPTER XIII

THE DAWN

(1)

THE darkness of the tragic night was over. The first faint streaks of dawn were stealthily and softly spreading over the eastern sky. It was a lovely dawn at Akkur.

The rising sun in all the impersonal glory and innocence of innate splendour, and in seeming ignorance of the tragic deeds overnight on this little planet, rose and moved above the circling clouds like a mandarin from his velvet bed of silk sheets. It benignly cast its first rays on Akkur, and did not seem to weep for the woes that had set in, all on a sudden, on the ancient house of Chockalinga. The hay-ricks and the grain-heaps high as hillocks that smiled welcome to the morning sun from generation to generation reared no more their heads in stately pride. The riches that gave the charm to Mr. Mudaliar's gay outlook on life were charred and reduced to mere heaps of coal-black ashes on which the sportive wind played scattering even the last traces of the ruin.

The garden house of Chockalinga, once gay and proud with the mellow ease of eleven generations of aristocratic peace and plenty, now looked the very picture of ruin, as if a clap of thunder had wiped it off in a tragic moment.

But hundreds of cottages ten miles around sang merrily the song of plenty with the heartiness of assured food for six months. But it was a song touched with a deep, hidden note of fear. The secret joy of stolen plenty was mixed with the acid tremor of anxiety. For, taking Nature's fruits, and fruits of your own toil, just for the moment held in the hands of another, vested by a strange law in the hands of an exploiting another, even to appease your own cruel calls of hunger, is a first-class crime against the sacred institution of property: the first of virtues in the animal kingdom becomes the first of sins in the ancient and honourable code of man.

(2)

The dawn saw the station-yard itself thronged to the full. The terrors of the night, the collision and the fire, told on every one. The railway station was instinctively thought of as the protector of all, as it linked the whole village to the world. The morning air was keen, and it refreshed the weary eyes that never closed in sleep the previous night.

Soon there was a rumbling sound on the railway track. Sundaram was ready and agile waving the green flag of welcome to the train. No. 5 with a new engine came stealing into the station punctually with a significant look, as it carried the transferred traffic from the Ceylon Boat Mail.

The Deputy-Collector of Mayavaram too travelled by the same train, as he thought it prudent to cultivate at once the new Collector even from the Mayavaram railway station. The vexed question of his promotion was pending settlement next quarter.

Rangan and Rajeswari, Ponnan and Padma too travelled by the same train. The scheduled stopping time at Akkur was just a minute.

But the collision and the fire and the Assistant Collector were events. Besides, the Assistant Collector should have enough time to have his morning coffee. Rangan, nothing at Egmore, was everything at Akkur; because in a wise moment he had sent beforehand a telegram from Madras to the Deputy-Collector at Mayavaram intimating his arrival.

(3)

" Mr. Mudaliar, why so early at the station ? Did the collision reach your ears and disturb your sleep ? " asked his friend, the Deputy-Collector, unaware of the prominent part played by this local magnate in the collision. " You look also very much wearied ; evidently you had no sleep overnight."

This poor Deputy-Collector, well versed in collection and audit to the last pie of the *kist*, and generally in all paper transactions, and the ablest hand at drafting revenue notes, had no idea of human nature in broad outline, of the extraordinary powers of sleep of Mr. Mudaliar.

"Nothing, sir, only some mischief has been played on me during my absence last evening, as I had feared so long. Kandan of whom I spoke to you is the root of the trouble: he is the arch-enemy of myself and your Government, sir. He is stirring these poor tillers of the soil to walk the path of fire, disturbing the peace and order of ages. Providence has sent you now most unexpectedly to my help. Look yonder, sir, all my hay-ricks and grain-heaps once high as hillocks were burnt down yesternight, twenty thousand *kalams* of paddy, all burnt or looted. Nay, I won't be sorry if all were burnt down, an offering to the God of fire for my sins in this and all my past lives. But this plunder by the hands of my own men who have eaten my salt for ages! With your help, sir, I propose to whip them till they disgorge every grain from their hiding places in their huts, or in their stomachs!"

Mr. Mudaliar was allowed the full length of his lament. For the Deputy-Collector kept on gazing at the excited crowd.

"Arson! that has attracted this crowd, I suppose; it's a serious offence under the Penal Code. Who did it actually, I wonder? Kandan at the bottom of this serious offence? Are you sure of it, Mr. Mudaliar? For all his culture and creed of non-violence, would he have stirred it himself? He might have preached some vague socialistic theories. But this burning of grain and hay-ricks, so dear to cattle and men, would he have been a direct party to loot, plunder, and fire? He talks sedition, there is no doubt about it; all his words and talks breathe fire and brimstone and he has a determined will."

Mr. Mudaliar interrupted in haste and said, "Kandan looks calm and gentle but he is full of fire like the *vanni* tree, and the lightest friction sets free the flame within."

"But it seems to me impossible, Mr. Mudaliar, that he has had a hand in this atrocious arson and plunder. In all my official life for twenty years this is the biggest loot I have known, twenty thousand *kalams* of paddy looted and burnt down in a single night; impossible to believe my eyes or ears!"

"But I'm sure, sir, that he is at the bottom of it all. It appears that even last evening at the toddy-shop he was inciting my men to do the final act of revenge to wipe out, as he fondly says often, the debt and sin of ages."

"In any event, if you are so sure of it, as you say you are, Mr. Mudaliar,—now that the new Collector *dorai* is here with us in the train on his way to Tranquebar, let us beg of him to stay for an hour in your garden-house and take his breakfast. Let him see the ruin himself, as no witness could convey it to him so well as his own eyes. That would indeed strengthen my hands to deal firmly with Kandan."

The Deputy-Collector paused a moment in thought and said in a really serious tone, "Kindly remember, Mr. Mudaliar, Kandan is no joke or trifle to play with. I understand he is very influentially supported, and he has friends all over; Madras, Delhi, and even London. And Mahatmaji is a great friend of Kandan. If we but touch him rashly, wires will fly all over the ends of the earth and questions will be put in the House of Commons and everywhere. However we shall invite the new Collector *dorai*, and feel the way."

"With pleasure, sir, then it is double luck to me for the day. Let the Collector come and stay with me not for one hour but for the whole year, and I'll make the garden-house fit to receive him."

"Very well, then, Mr. Mudaliar, you've the Auburn car ready with you now?"

"Well, there it is, ready to start at your wish."

A little far away from the entrance under the rising mound and shade of a cocoanut tree stood the Auburn car in all its pristine glory of colour in the radiant morning sun. An urchin, as if he had overheard the conversation, sounded the bellowing horn once, twice, thrice, for the sheer joy of it.

The Deputy-Collector with his awkward gait and shuffling trousers—the only occasion on which he draped himself in his old age in the European style to please his masters, moved fast like a circus elephant, to where Rangan and Rajeswari were seated in the train, to explain the trifling change in the programme.

"May it please your honour, I understand that the arrangements at Tranquebar are not yet ready to receive your honour and her ladyship in proper style. May it please you to breakfast here at Akkur. This is Mr. Chockalinga Mudaliar, the President of the Taluk Board and a member of the District Board, and the leading *mirasdar* of this Taluk. He owns about two thousand acres and pays the heaviest *kist* in our Taluk, if not in the whole District. He has a beautiful garden-house near-by. Your honoured self and her ladyship may rest a while there after the hard journey overnight. Then in the evening your honour may drive to Tranquebar by the Auburn Sedan."

"We are entirely in your hands, Mr. Deputy-Collector," Rangan uttered the words loftily, swallowing half of them in a splendid yawn, though the capacious mouth of Rangan frightened Rajeswari a little.

The Deputy-Collector turned to Sundaram who was standing near-by reverentially.

"Then, station-master, you may send out the train. We go by car to Tranquebar."

Rangan and Rajeswari gladly got down from the train, and moved towards the exit, fussed about by liveried peons in front. Rangan innocently took the crowd as having come to pay their respects to the new Collector even at so early dawn. He already thought that the Deputy-Collector though very unpromising in appearance like himself was a capable man, a man of deeds.

(4)

" Is it you, Kanda? What an unexpected delight to see you even before we have set foot in your place! We were just thinking of you for long while in the train, and our very thoughts seem to have indeed brought you here to this station," Rajeswari greeted Kandan before they had advanced even a few steps from the train. Rajeswari's eagle eyes caught Kandan in the crowd, and Kandan's presence could be easily missed nowhere.

" Is it you, Rajee? Imposssible to believe my own eyes!" exclaimed Kandan in wonder half extricating himself from the crowd.

There was a smile of calm, spreading joy in Kandan's face quite vying with the tranquil charm of the early dawn. And Rajeswari stood rooted to the spot full of sap—the old, old love flooding her bosom like mountain floods that fill the river-valleys in the fulfilling monsoon hour, foaming and churning, lisping and eddying, and moving even rocks and trees on the way.

"Is it you, Kanda? What a joy to meet you so unexpectedly!" Rangan exclaimed with sincerity. For, the memory of many fine days spent together at Oxford before they met Rajeswari on a fateful day on a common platform came to him in a flood. Rangan shook hands with Kandan to the wonder of the crowd and the dismay of Mr. Mudaliar. They even went to the unusual length of a hearty half-embrace. So full of final ease and tranquillity was Kandan that even Rangan's materialistic mind felt its charm and influence.

Sincerity carries with it the healing touch of the gods, It is the very amber from which the first electrons of a spiritual life are generated. It is the focussing lens of life—the base of all *Yoga* that leads to final communion with the All-knowing. Sincerity is *tapas*.

(5)

It was a critical moment for Sundaram. Rangan's face had a strange, far-off familiar look. He ran to his hut. "Sarasu, it seems to me your brother,—the new Collector just arrived. You know I've seen him but once for less than an hour now many years ago at our wedding. Come out and see."

Sarasvati came out with a palpitating heart. She had not seen her brother now for nearly five years, and not heard from him at all for over three. She moved like a faery queen to the station-yard. All eyes were turned on her. Rangan made her out at once. A moment of false pride just stood in the way for a fleeting second. But the glory of Sarasvati's full-blown beauty and her looks of celestial grace cleared the ground for recognition. The brother's love triumphed immediately over the Collector's pride. He greeted her warmly with eyes glowing with fraternal love.

" Sarasu, forgive me for these many years of silence and neglect. I feel it now a crime ; I haven't even written to you these years."

" Dear Ranga, should you write to me ? A brother's love is brother's love with or without pen and ink and postage. It's enough you have remembered me. Not a day passed without my thinking of you and of our dear father and mother who havn't lived long enough to see you so high in life."

" It is our ill-luck. Are you here, dear Sarasu, waiting for the train ? "

" I'm always here, waiting for trains."

" I don't understand you."

" I'm the wife of the station-master of Akkur."

Sarasvati did not drop her eyelids or wrinkle her brow. There was a serene calm in her voice.

Rangan was covered with confusion for a moment. But he quickly added, " You'll be no more that, dear Sarasu. I'm proud of you. You have blossomed like the lotus in the little pond of my family and we are proud of you. Would my mother could come back to-day for an hour, if only to see the pearl of you for a second! I'm blessed in a sister like you, dear Sarasu."

Rangan and Sarasvati moved on together a little away from the crowd. Kandan and Rajee followed them silently with thoughts of their own. Slowly they reached the Auburn car waiting for them like a state elephant.

To Rajeswari's surprise Ponnan too was standing near the stately bonnet of the Auburn Sedan, gracefully and humbly bowing to all the four. To Sarasvati's surprise Kamakshi too was following her. Such was the bond of friendship forged overnight in the hour of distress.

"What, Ponna, you too have got down at Akkur. Why not at Tranquebar?" Rajeswari asked.

"Madam, hereafter my life is cast with you. I'm your humble servant in the national cause. Even if you reject me, spurn me, I must die only at your feet and take my salvation therefrom." Padma nodded assent. For, Ponnan and Padma had already become deeply interested in each other.

Faithful Ponnan and heroic Padma were made the fifth and the sixth and Kamakshi the seventh. All the seven drove in the spacious Auburn Sedan to Mr. Mudaliar's garden-house racing at forty miles an hour. For the road was in excellent condition beautifully metalled. If not at least that, what is a President of a Taluk Board worth who has under his control a lakh of rupees earmarked for metalling roads in his Taluk?

As for the Deputy-Collector and Mr. Mudaliar, they followed the illustrious guests to the car, gracefully nodding approval at every step all the way, and wondering at Kandan's amazing turn of luck and Sarasvati's beauty. They fell behind for a second trip in the car, and they had plenty of time to explain and adjust this mystery tale of wonder about Rangan and Sarasvati.

Sundaram acted as the interpreter of this mystic story, being Sarasvati's wedded lord. He claimed before the unbelieving audience that the new Collector was his own brother-in-law. As for Kandan he spun as good a story as a plausible piecing of things together could make, that they were perhaps friends at college in London.

But Kandan's intimacy with the new Collector seemed to Mr. Mudaliar the death-knell to all his fond hopes of revenge and destruction. Still the Deputy-Collector cheered him with a whispered word that the initiative in matters of law and order lay with him, and that the British touch to the Indian Penal Code made the law of the land no respector of persons. Law would take its own unswerving course; of course, eventually for the benefit of the great Mr. Mudaliar, the lord of two thousand acres and the leading *mirasdar* of the Taluk who paid the heaviest *kist* to the Government.

Besides, the Deputy-Collector's only daughter's marriage was fixed for the day the next fortnight, and Mr. Mudaliar's co-operation would be invaluable in conducting to a fine success this heavy, taxing, social function.

Is it not that in such touching mutuality life's most sacred record of intimate pleasures are secreted like honey in honeycombs in inaccessible rock-crevices in high ranges of hills?

Mr. Mudaliar lavished with the easy spendthrift grace of a born nobleman, the wealth, gathered grain by grain with ant-like industry, by hundreds of his own *pannaials* in the mud and mire of the fields.

What does it matter to an impersonal divinity that choice flowers distil the honey from the dew by a mysterious process still unknown to man, that bees roam for miles to gather the honey drop by drop with infinite toil, and at last bring together this intricate work of worship to the Sun-God, and build the honeycomb amidst sun-lit rocks, patted by the roaming wind, blessed by the murmuring brook and kissed by the stars,—all only to be broken at the end by the heavy and plundering footsteps of man?

CHAPTER XIV

NEELAKSHI'S PLIGHT

(1)

KIND reader, we have to go back a little to the earlier events of this story and trace the fortune of Neelakshi the previous night just about the time of Padma's precipitate flight.

The twilight had just darkened a little relieving the clear purity of the crescent moon on the auspicious *panchami* day. Next to Padma, the last-born, Neelakshi loved tenderly the eldest son of Raghu, the heir apparent to her hopes and dreams who assured her the continuance of her line. Chandru, the five-year-old boy, lean, lithe, handsome, and active as a lance in the hour of play, was mercilessly worrying Neelakshi's disturbed mind with many probing questions of curiosity natural to a child on very many common things. He showed a precocious incisiveness in the pursuit of his enquiries.

" Mother, tell me, tell me at once or I'll break this slate upon your head till I get an answer. Why did you scold uncle Padma so hard this evening, mother? What's wrong in uncle going about in the crowd shouting "Gandhiki jai"? But for your anger, I too should have joined the crowd and my uncle, and danced away the evening by the Uppanar river."

"Chandru, you may play for a while on the sand in the cool evening hour; you are quite a little child. But Padma is a grown up boy who has got to finish his school course this year sitting for the public examination in a month or so. He can't afford to waste his time—tom-fooling like this!"

"Mother, why should children go to school, sit still, study and listen hard and bear the endless hardship of a teacher or an examination, even on a rainy day when nature's call is all for play out in the open—tracing the flow of rain-water from one little pool to another, and roaming in wet sand from one little mound to another."

"Child, man is born to work on this earth so that he may earn his food, and work we should all must, even you, each in his own allotted way; in a few months, Chandru, you too will be put to school."

"And carry pencil, paper, and slate in a *khaddar* bag and take the chance of the teacher's cane! Never." Chandru shuddered even as he spoke and asked again, after a moments' seeming pause of reflection, "Mother, you say all of us are born to work for our food, but mother, how does going to school bring us rice and dholl, milk and ghee, and all the sweetmeats you give me. You have yourself said so often that it is work in the fields and tending cows on the meadows by river-banks that bring us these dainties for our food. Tell me, mother, what has slate and pencil to do with sweetmeats and what gain it is to the sense of pleasure to go to school and sit in a crowd trembling before a pox-faced, oldish man with a cane longer than his right hand."

"Dear boy, these are questions far beyond your age, whose answers you can never understand till you are yourself put to school. Chandru, pray, you are a good boy, don't hold that slate like that as if you are going to smash it on me any moment."

"No, no, mother, never will I go to school; Chandru will never go to school, to that little jail where you can't play or even talk while the cane lies idly on the table. I'll rather roam in the streets, and play with calves and puppies; I'll spend my time on river banks, throwing blades of grass or flowers into the stream or climbing the tallest tree for the sheer joy of height or join Gandhiji and shout with the crowd, 'Mahatmajiki jai'. Sure, mother, Chandru will never go to school, take it from me, mother." Chandru spoke in an assured voice and with a strange maturity far above his years.

The parcel express thundered along the Uppanar bridge and the low, heavy, grinding, rolling sound of motion over a massive iron bridge was heard distinctly in the Brahmins' street of Shiyali where Neelakshi lived resting her dreams of a great future on Raghu and Padma.

Chandru listened to the distant rumbling motion of the train slightly pricking his ears and whistling a tune as if he longed for an untasted joy.

"Mother, I long to see a train in motion and take a joy ride to Kumbakonam. Let us go and see new places. Won't you take me out one day. *Appa* is always in office late in the night and never returns home before I go to sleep. Will you take me out tomorrow morning, mother, on a trip in train to some place or I'll myself run away to Coleroon."

Chandru spoke with infinite decision in his infant voice. His eyes flashed with the approaching joy of an unknown delight and his cheeks flushed with impatience. Chandru's, even more than Padma's, was a truant's soul, the truant who loves freedom as the very breath of his life—the stuff with which both the hero and the unknown volunteer in any nation's fight for freedom is made.

"Chandru, I'm not surprised. Your uncle Padma at your age talked like this, and no wonder the nephew takes after the youngest colt in the family." Neelakshi smiled beneficently on Chandru more pleased than alarmed by his bold, prankish words. She seemed a moment lost in thought. Stroking Chandru's cheeks affectionately, she said with a little sigh, "It is 7.30 now and Padma has not yet come home."

Neelakshi had hardly uttered these words when she heard, "Neelakshi, you always laughed at my boy," shouted in a shrill voice a middle-aged widow ascending the steps of Neelakshi's house, who had long borne her a grudge for having spoken once lightly in public of her boy's ability.

"My boy, Kittu," she continued in the same shrill voice, "My boy, Kittu has been selected for the examination—the headmaster is a kind and good man. What about Padma, you know, Neela?"

"Has the list been put up?" Neelakshi anxiously asked.

"Yes, don't you know, Neela, quite an hour ago—I hear that Padma—but you had better verify."

"Padma's name is not in the selected list?" Neela both asked and replied to herself. The maternal bosom heaved in doubt, the pale cheeks flushed with anger and uncertainty.

"That's what I hear—" was the indifferent and studiedly revengeful, shrill voice of the middle-aged widow who had just waited her chance for this hour of spite.

Neelakshi heard the thunder clap, and seemed to faint for a moment. But she soon gathered her presence of mind only to be troubled once again by another uncertain fear, "That's why perhaps my darling Padma has not yet come home?"

Chandru carelessly took up the question and answered it with a truant prophecy in his voice, "I am sure, mother, Padma will never come back home. For, mother, you were very hard on him this evening. He has left us all for ever, to roam the world over like a free boy. How I wish I could join my uncle and wander with him for ever in pathless tracks in jungles and winding foot-line by the side of streams."

Chandru pulled his grandmother by the right arm as if in despair to draw her attention to himself and said, "Mother take it from me, I'll never go to a school nor carry pencil, slate or books."

Chandru, the boy of five spoke in accents of untutored innocence, playfully but with a sureness and freedom that come of primary feelings and a natural approach to life.

None loves the freedom of the open sky more than the boys and girls whom we slowly reduce to mass serfdom in schools, and break them to hard and weary work so that when they become tamed as citizens the riches of the few rich may be mounded into higher heaps by the slaving hands and anguished hearts of the million poor. Chandru's infant words of charm and revolt were but echoes gathered of the song of freedom vibrant in the air of renascent India.

(2)

When Padma was lecturing on the sandy bed of the Uppanar river, Raghu had to go once again to office on an urgent call from the Tahsildar. Suddenly the news came that the Deputy Collector was expected to visit the Taluk Office in the course of that week on the usual round of inspection. Both the Tahsildar and Raghu anticipated a troubled time ahead as the Deputy Collector carried with him a great reputation for severe handling of his subordinates and a complete mastery of revenue details. And he was of the hard-to-please variety, a vague terror to the subordinate staff. Raghu faced the prospect by harder work at the desk and a deeper conviction that all his work was sterile and did nobody any good except the fellows at the top who drew a nice salary. After two hours of hard work by pale kerosene light spilling unfiltered ink on brown and yellowish paper, and scattering black sand in lieu of blotting, Raghu returned home later than usual that night.

"Mother, has Padma come home? I feel a strange tremor of heart," Raghu entered the house, speaking to his mother who was sitting on the pial anxiously awaiting the return of Padma and Raghu.

"Why so very late to-day? unusually late, Raghu,—hard work in the office?"

"Hard and dry work indeed, mother, to feed this capitalistic society, to make the rich richer and the poor poorer. Mother, I'm disgusted with the work. Why, Padma has not yet returned? It's past eight."

"Padma has not returned, may not return at all—he has not been sent up for the exam. If you are not quite tired, Raghu, will you now go and see the headmaster and find out if it is true?"

Raghu immediately left the house and returned an hour later, just to declare in a word, "Mother,

Padma is completely lost to us. That sensitive boy will never more return home."

So long as Padma was at home burdening Raghu's wife with extra work—Neelakshi ceased toiling by the kitchen-fire ever since her daughter-in-law came home—Raghu felt his own younger brother a thorn that made his steps painful and uneasy. But the scene of the evening and the fact of separation proved a crucial moment of change. For, the compassion of blood relationship was kindled in the adverse hour.

Raghu refused to dine that night, but sat reading by the light of a smoking lamp Maxim Gorky's *Mother.* Neelakshi having failed to persuade Raghu to dine, herself took a copy of the *Mahabaratha* and opened the volume where the great fight of Kurukshetra begins.

Chandru generally slept with his father in the same bed, and he had already gone to sleep. Every half hour he began to lisp a call for his father, spreading his sleeping hands in searching embrace. Raghu lifted his eyes from Gorky's *Mother*, lingered a loving while on his boy's fine features from head to foot, tucked a pillow into the empty embrace, patted the sleeping boy gently on the back, and returned with a refreshed zeal to Gorky's *Mother*. Neelakshi too stopped poring over the battle scenes of the *Mahabaratha* which kept harmony with the tumult of her heart and ambitions, and drank in the scene of her son's devotion to his son.

Chandru turned again in his bed and called this time for his grandmother. Raghu responded to the call while Neela gazed on. The father patted to sleep the lotus softness of his boy's legs, long, lithe and tender like a plantain shoot in the glorious monsoon hour. He was struck, while the boy was asleep, with Chandru's close likeness of features to Padma. And a paternal sweat of anxiety for a distant unknown future gathered on his brow. Even in the midst of pain Neelakshi's maternal bosom was flooded with joy for a moment at the sight of his son stroking the tender feet of Chandru, only to be wiped out the next minute by thoughts of absent Padma whom Chandru so much resembled in the sleeping hour.

CHAPTER XV

THE AFTERMATH

(1)

THE *paracheri* of Akkur had a sleepless and disturbed though eventful night. But the dawn found them broken up into knots studded all over, discussing the consequences of their predatory adventure overnight. But daylight brought in a strange cowardice to these looting lions by the night. Nandan, Mookkan, and Katteri, Irullan, Karuppan, and Irullappan were immersed in the possibilities of revenge and punishment.

"*Anne,* Katteri," Karuppan came running to Katteri's cottage in the *paracheri*, "Did I not tell you yesterday even at the toddy-shop—we may be uncontrolled masters for the night but with the dawn we'll be prisoners surrounded by red-turbaned police fellows. Look yonder, there goes our *pannai* motorcar, hooting and roaring on its way. See closely, it doesn't carry our *yejaman* but a load of police chiefs and their wives. The great collector *dorai* has perhaps come, and all will soon be over with us: our *paracheri* will be in chains."

"I fear so, *anne*, my right eye throbbed when I brought the looted paddy in—my wife sneezed ill-omen. Let us act together before it is too late. What do you say, Nandan *anne*."

"Say all that you have to say and finish your speech," Nandan spoke with indifference.

"Before it is too late—before all come and surround us with red turban, long bayonets and handcuffs—let us take, basket by basket, the plundered paddy, and drop it in yonder ocean-like tank, consign it to the silence of the voiceless waters—the paddy will stand two days' drowning, and then we can take it out like divers diving for pearls—boil it, husk it, and then make it our own when it can tell no tale!"

"A nice idea if done overnight, but can we do it all now in broad daylight?"

"Why not, a line of cocoanut and mango trees screen our way to the tank; we can march under cover one by one. But it must be done at once—in half-an-hour they will swarm us here, after they have had their coffee, like vultures over a dying plough-bull."

"Fie, fie upon your plan," Katteri thundered. "I loathe to hear a coward's voice from among you to-day—you, who raged like a lion and worked like an elephant yesternight, should advise us like this! Let him who can fight us, arrest us, imprison us, be he police or *tahsil*—he can reach Katteri's cottage only by walking over his dead body."

A great tumult issued and many voices were heard in council. At last it was decided that discretion was far better than valour in broad daylight, and it was perilous to stock so much of looted paddy with an army of police hot on scent,—the young master having returned home and in a frenzy of anger at the loss of so much money and prestige.

In half an hour, gunny bag after gunny bag, basket after basket of paddy grains, ripe and golden yellow, sank into the bottom mire of the tank only to make a gala day for fish, young and old, short and long.

The famished hands of the pariah women helped greatly in this voluntary surrender to the silence of Nature. The piteous cries of starving children, lean, lanky and ill-covered with a bare loin-cloth of rags rang to the skies, "*Appa*, *appa*, give us a handful of grains so that we may husk them on our own tender palms and eat them raw and fresh."

Strangely comes the stern rebuke of the father who becomes a beast in the degrading struggle of fear born of poverty. For, the fresh husks of fine table-rice never given to these tillers of the soil for wages, found scattered near the cottages, might be detected by the keen eyes of the police and the guilt of loot fixed beyond doubt.

(2)

Rangan and Rajeswari, had delicious Polson's coffee, in Mr. Mudaliar's bangalow, after a preliminary stroll and chat for an hour in the garden. Then it was agreed that Rangan and the Deputy Collector should make an informal visit to the *paracheri* and hold a non-official enquiry. Chockalinga was left out to enable Rangan to carry on an independent investigation and it was also suggested that Mr. Mudaliar would find it difficult to control his temper before his very men who committed the loot. Padma begged of Kandan to allow him to follow the group to the *paracheri*. To Padma used to the ugliness and rubbish-heaps of semi-urban Shiyali, the rural scenes of Akkur seemed a perfect paradise.

Soon the beautiful Auburn Sedan stood at the threshold of the *paracheri*. Rangan and the Deputy Collector, Kandan and Padma, alighted and stood for a while, each viewing the scattered huts with an emotion of his own.

" It's a difficult job for you, Ranga, even for an informal investigation. Law lies clearly one way; humanity quite another," Kandan broke the grim silence of the investigating party.

" You fellows, bring out the stolen paddy or the whole *paracheri* will be thrashed, arrested, and put in jail," roared the Deputy Collector in the fullness of his magisterial power before the very eyes of his superior officer. He had already ordered for a posse of constables from Tranquebar, to give Rangan a taste of his foresight and ability in case of trouble.

"*Yejaman, yejaman,*" Nandan, Mookkan, and Irullan bellowed in one voice of entreaty, "we are all as innocent as these children by whose head we swear." Callous to all finer sentiments by centuries of serfdom, spoke the voice of Fear that always throbbed in the heart and rattled in the throat of the pariah.

"Sorakkai Tevan, the ancient enemy of the *pannai*," Nandan said in a deliberate voice of feigned truthfulness so that he might discharge the patriarchal duty of protecting his clan in an hour of peril, "had looted last night our garden, our granary, and our fair name when *yejaman* had been away, and we, his pariahs, were lost in an empty brawl at the toddy shop, and later on, alas, we were all away to a neighbouring village to see some stupid, little, street-play, sitting all through night like an owl, chattering and chewing pan."

Nandan, the aged veteran leader implored with vigour and persuasiveness and swore solemnly, "In the name of my grandfather, I'll restore to-night to my *yejaman* all the twenty thousand *kalams* of paddy burnt to ashes by our enemies' fire—plundered by rats when the cat was away. I'll bring to *dorai's* feet, Sorakkai Tevan and the whole of his family, hand and foot bound." Nandan made an impassioned vow.

Rangan unconsciously touched his hat as if in graceful acknowledgment of the compliment paid to the power of his presence.*

Mookkan shook and circled his head in approval, his eagle nose keenly cutting and soaring against the morning sun, and his animated hands vigorously gesticulating revenge.

Katteri who was all for violence somewhere, shouted approval, "That's a nice idea—we'll do it to-night, Collector Saheb. Sorakkai Tevan will pay measure for measure as penalty, and we'll leave this time no trace of himself or of his *pannai*. We'll bring on our backs—men, women and children—all the thirty thousand *kalams* of paddy, old and new, in his acre-wide granary and prove before the dawn of another day that we are true to the salt we have eaten for generations."

Rangan, led by the heavy-shaped but animated Deputy Collector, was getting more and more absorbed in the official run of mind, and fancied that he was really investigating a case on duty with all the resources of the British Empire behind his little finger. His mind easily took in the office-bit like a well-worked draught horse.

Kandan saw the tragedy of the situation at one glance, the vast drama that was being enacted there before his very eyes. To Padma, a true lover of all truant ways, who read at school less of his books and more of his class-fellows, it was a ripe hour for him to push ahead his age by years.

Kandan and Padma fell into an eager conversation, while Rangan began unconsciously to take notes in right earnest. The Deputy Collector showed the utmost vigilance and zeal in distinguishing himself happily before his superior officer.

"Sir, look at these children of the soil," Padma spoke in earnest to Kandan, "famished and in rags, in dirt and in poverty,—and look at the Auburn Sedan at the very threshold of the *paracheri*," Padma flared up in juvenile anger and pity.

"An eloquent contrast—pursue the line of enquiry Padma,—I like very much your wise, boyish mind, the innocence that is always near Truth, therefore nearer Reality—."

"Thank you very much, sir—do they not say that a car means Rs. 150 a month, and to Mr. Mudaliar's generous life, it must cost him all told, at least Rs. 300 a month, to maintain his stately Sedan." Padma spoke like an expert in the line, and Kandan listened to him with a benignant face encouraging him by a nod to continue.

"Three hundreds a month!" Padma began a new line of thought. "What a miracle you cannot achieve with this princely gift in the humble life of these pariahs! This *paracheri* can be changed into a paradise. You can work and feed on the most generous scale twenty families, or employ for ever twenty teachers to teach the way to live a decent life to these ignorant, little boys and girls in all grades of dirt and disease, that now crowd round us wondering at the car. How long, sir, you think the system has been vicious like this?—or will it endure for ever?"

"Padma, some of these things live the longest on our long ailing earth—it has been so for a very long time. But under the strenuous ache of modern life it is working great hardship. Skilled labour is honoured with a surplus gift of money, and unskilled labour which produces the true wealth of the world is coldly treated with a handful of rice so that the body may be kept alive for to-morrow's toil."

"Yes, sir, the whole system must be smashed and a new world be built for all, where freedom and equality shall be the base of life."

"Yes, Padma, the social freedom to grow as the native bias in each inclines each, and the economic equality and chance to win the day's bread with minimum toil on lines of work each as he pleases. Life is unequal, Padma, evolution works unequal. That seems to be the remorseless law of life. All I crave for is economic equality and no chance for one to exploit another."

"That's a noble ideal, sir. It expresses clearly what I have long been longing for. Teach me to work under you, sir. I'll follow you to death—I can't bear the sight of so much inequality, so much social injustice,—it is good for neither, twenty thousand *kalams* per annum for one man to enjoy, and to all those around him nothing but hard and dull over-work day in, day out, and a measure of rice just to keep alive the body so that it may do more work for the morrow. Alas, sir, is it so all over the world?"

"Yes, Padma, it is so all over the world, but here in our land the shock of modern impact from the west has come all too close and sudden—our men do lack a great many civic and social virtues which temper the new misery in other climes. Our old moorings have snapped, and we have not yet found the new. To gain freedom and peace and perfect our social order once again we must work hard and build a new tradition on old, old foundations. You are young and enquiring, patriotic and pure,—Padma, consecrate your life generously to this work. Your sons and grandsons will then tell a different tale."

Already a group of little, pariah boys and girls surrounded Kandan and Padma, and begged of them respectfully from at a distance, with salaaming hands and twinkling eyes that spoke the language of suffering. Padma put his hand into his pocket and remembered painfully that only a few hours ago he travelled in train without a ticket for lack of copper. Kandan saw Padma's awkwardness at a glance, and placed quietly a few silver and copper pieces in Padma's hands. Padma scattered them to the amazed children who, picking them up, scampered off, not believing their own eyes and their good-luck for the day.

Rangan still continued taking notes of evidence of Nandan, Mookkan, and Katteri, Irullan, Karuppan, and Irullappan, and Nochi, the *talayari*; and Govindan, Pavadai, and Nallan.

CHAPTER XVI

TRANQUEBAR, THE QUEEN OF THE COROMANDEL COAST

(1)

TRANQUEBAR, the Queen of the Coromandel Coast, is now but an old, dilapidated lady, wrinkled with the ruin of age. But she must have been once a thing of beauty, judging from the shapely, bird-like outline of her features.

Tranquebar is finely situated at the mouth of the river Veerasholan, a branch of the Cauvery, on a rising ground of sand-dunes right on the very edge of the sea and the foam of the waves. Cocoanut gardens, mango groves, and banana plantations grow luxuriantly, throwing all over a solemn shade of green when the noon-day sun sparkles on the glittering sea.

Tranquebar has a history that dates back two thousand years to the spacious days of King Karikalan. It then marked the extreme southern limits of the ancient city of Puhar which lay ten miles square, like a mighty eagle that had spread its wings on the ground just before its final flight to the sky.

The Danes in their brief hour of power built a fort three centuries ago on the foreshore lashed by the very waves they had ridden over, dolphin-like, on the sea. The fort has an antique appearance. It now stands slightly remodelled for use as a rest-house for the less valorous but better paid army of civil servants under the Crown. And it was placed by special order, for a fortnight, at the exclusive use of Rangan, the new Assistant Collector.

(2)

A week had passed after their arrival at Tranquebar, and only a few days more remained for Rangan to join duty at Tanjore as Assistant Collector. But his state of mind was indescribable. Rajeswari Bai had quietly resolved to work for the public cause in her own way, unmoved by the pitiful entreaties of Rangan not to walk the path of fire and imperil a safe and happy future. But she pleaded in return the cause of the country with such sincerity and courage that the patriotic call went home direct to his heart. So Rangan stood painfully divided between two loyalties.

But it seemed illogical and difficult to Rangan to make the sacrifice it meant, especially after having tasted the sweets of office for a couple of years. Could he heroically, at the bidding of Rajee, put an end voluntarily to a career that might end in something big some day? And even in this struggle of mind his love for Rajeswari doubled itself.

The sea breeze had set in very early that day, even at three. The waves were slowly gaining ground. The mid-day lull of the sea was over. The old Danish fort was standing in all its antique glory just in front of the sea, as if waiting patiently for another sea-song from the restless blue. It seemed to stand in a pensive mood as if watching for a chance to complete its interrupted history.

The crabs were moving quickly to and fro on the shore, backwards and forwards, up and down, from land to sea, from sea to land. The waves went on with their ceaseless work, washing the sands of the shore in lisping worship, polishing them to marble smoothness and beauty, and filling the crab-holes with bubbling spouts of water and rings of foam.

To the south lay the Veerasholan with a mile stretch of sand at its mouth. In monsoon time it would be one roaring rush of plenty. But now the river was a slender blue ribbon of brine that ran from sea to land winding up like a sea-serpent on deep sand.

The breeze was blowing in gusts and had not yet steadied into a silent sweep. The creaking old windows and doors of the Danish fort were jamming against their framework and rusty hinges as if longing for the freedom of the wind and the sea. The glass panes shivered and trembled in the wild breeze. The big open quadrangle of the fort lay in the very middle of the walled-in space and gave a luxurious look of opulence to this old building of three hundred years, now bandaged here and there with new belts of cement.

The fort is full of low-cellared rooms, and the ceiling in many places almost grazes the head with a touch of humility. But there is one fascinating turret shooting high into the sky against the suggestive background of the infinite sea. Daring lads climb it for a full view of Nature all around,—an open turret to which you go meandering amidst cracked domes. It is the proper spying place, calm and lovely, to catch the sea and the river in all the natural beauty of their mingling hour.

(3)

It was five o'clock in the evening and the sun had already declined far into the west. Rangan and Sarasvati were in the open turret. Kandan and Rajeswari were on lèvel sand in the ever-disputed frontier between the land and the sea. They were standing at ease with the waves gently laving their feet.

In harmony with the lisping murmur of the sea Kandan spoke in a gentle, pensive voice: "Rajee, there's indeed a divinity that shapes our ends. The seeming woes of the day nourish within them the weal for the morrow. In the most tragic hour of my life when I thought everything was lost, my freedom, my name, my work, and sure I was I was a doomed man, your miraculous appearance has saved me."

"You feared the arson would be put on your head—even now anything may happen if Rangan resigns his job."

"Rangan resigns his job! You mean it, Rajee?"

"Yes, I've asked him to—he may—and join us in our humble work. Kanda, I learnt to value you only after you had left us at London,—so grave, wistful, and loving that memories of you came flooding up in happy reminiscence. The loss to the Civil Service has become a gain to true Service. Such a birth as yours is a blessing to our stricken land."

"There are, Rajee, hundreds and thousands of such workers like myself in this country—the unknown volunteer who has risked his life and liberty in the struggle for Swaraj when the call of the Mother came. Why do you single me out? Mine is nothing but a response to the common call in the air. But yours, Rajee, is the finest sacrifice in the history of our chequered land. How high-born ladies like you, fed in luxury, have answered to the call of the Mother and sacrificed everything! This is truly selfless and rare indeed."

"Kanda, our work is nothing compared with yours. We simply follow in towns the beaten track, cheered to the echo by the mob and praised to the skies by head-lines in the press—and that rewards the heart which longs for praise in return for public work. But yours is the work of the saint, lofty, detached, lonely, courting no publicity and rating selfless work its own and only reward. And then you work at the very base of Indian life, the village, clearing the silt and slime of ages by diving deep and risking life, while we simply work at the top lazily gathering together the urban scum and the idle foam that floats thereon. Accept me as your humble co-worker, so that I may spend the rest of my life with you forever."

Kandan was deeply moved by the sincerity of her words. "I must say this, now or never, Rajee; words that come welling deep from my heart. I've been reading in the papers of your courage and sacrifice at Bombay—little did I dream that you would so soon be near me—can you measure me now, how proud and tall I feel! Little do you know—for it's a secret with my Maker,—even this little work I'm doing here is your chance gift to me—"

"My gift!"

"Yes, your gift, Rajee, devoted work for a sacred public cause comes not to all and sundry—unless one's soul is stirred by some sublime stir. And Rajee, you remember those fervent days of mine—"

A wave came trembling all the way from mid-ocean and broke in flowery kisses at the foam-embroidered feet of Rajee.

A blush reddened her cheeks.

"When I was head over ears in love with you, dear Rajee, when every nerve of my being sang the strange music of the gods, and the aspiring flesh tingled with a creative joy, and when I knew that you could never return it, though you pitied me for my seeming virtues,—virtues that never go to bring a woman to a man's feet, as you yourself so gently hinted—the words are still ringing, for they have made my future life and plan of action,—Rangan drew you so well to himself with his fine speeches—it seemed for a day as if I would go mad, and indeed I was mad for a day."

Rajee was so profoundly absorbed in the story that she did not feel even a dashing wave which had nearly drenched them both with the sea water.

"But, thanks to my forefathers, and thanks to you who stirred me with the sublime churn of love. Like a heavy cloud burdened with unshed waters, which descends as rain at the touch of wind my higher self was liberated by a mere look from you. All my thoughts of disappointed love for you turned into a consecrated love for my Motherland. I resolved at once to sail for India after a fortnight's stay in Natal. The I.C.S. without you seemed to me the poorest thing in the world—and I threw it up as a toy—Rangan and myself would have never cared to sit for the I.C.S.—we were meant for the law and public affairs—but we thought that the I.C.S. was the only way to win your aristocratic love. So, Rajee, once again life has become sweeter to me, life lived on dreams of unrest and honest work every day for the weal of the humbler folk. In the starlit sky under the ever-fresh and wind-swept sand-dunes, sweetest thoughts of you pillowed me every night to sleepless sleep."

Kandan sank on the wet sand almost exhausted by the emotion these thoughts had stirred in him.

"Well, dear Kanda, sometimes we treasure the very things we have first been careless about,—after we've lost them for ever. Well, these very thoughts of you must have brought me all the way from the Arabian sea to the Bay of Bengal. I'm sure, I felt similarly, though Rangan is still attached to me,—and I to him in a way—"

"Rangan still only attached to you!"

To hear from her own lips that she had not yet been married gave him a strange freedom and relief. Not that he hoped that Rajee would ever become his own, but it was something that Rajee was still free as a bird to sing a song of her own and act as she chose for the country's cause.

"The love of the Mother, Kanda, the grand passion for my country fills my being and floods my heart night and day, like the sea that ebbs and flows into the little creek at the mouth of the river. I must work for the freedom of my country first; for which I must have my own freedom. This is the most fateful time, now or never."

"These are just my thoughts as well, Rajee. I've consecrated my life for the service of the country, in your own holy name, and I repeat the vow at your feet in the presence of the sacred sea and the sun."

And Kandan stood mute for a while as if lost in prayer, in communion with the All-High. Then he slowly turned to the west as if to see the glory of the setting sun. He saw Rangan and Sarasvati standing in the open turret of the fort.

"Look yonder, Rajee, turn this side. Rangan and Sarasvati seem like Lilliputians from the lofty height of that open turret. And Sarasvati has a star-like beauty—"

"Rather say a moon-like beauty—and Sarasvati shines softly so much like the moon, and Rangan is so nearly like the cloud in the moon—"

"Yes, Rajee, how unlike they are for brother and sister!"

"Yes, how unlike they are—a very mild way, Kanda, of stating facts that stare one in the face."

Rajee's eyes beamed with a strange lustre.

"But Sarasvati is a wonder to us in many ways, Kanda. The Feminine has reached perfection in her: gentle and sweet as a fawn in play but decided and powerful in her views and work. There's a mysterious charm in her voice and a cosmic quiet in her eyes. There is a healing touch in her words and a rhythmic song in the very air she breathes in and out. I'm sure, it's the result of a perfect cycle of lives, devoted, pure, simple, and true. She's just the Eternal Feminine that would go to make causes great by a mere look or word of blessing, and keep the freedom of man from being sold. She has given me an angel's strength by her nod."

Kandan and Rajeswari were already feeling a friendship far greater and nobler than the tie that love of the flesh twists in its most frenzied or ambitious hour. They were already feeling the spiritual bond of a higher union as if they both belonged to some ancient *sanyasin* order working for the uplift of the fallen race of man and the evolution of a new order of life.

(4)

Ponnan approached Kandan and Rajeswari in solemn, measured steps, roughing the sands as if counting the grains like a child that was just having its allotted five minutes for play. Ponnan was now their trusted servant especially after his relationship with Kandan was verified. All suspicions of him were set at rest.

Ponnan took out a telegram from his pocket and asked, "Where's the Collector *dorai*, madam? Here's a telegram for him."

"Collector *dorai*, Ponna, has disappeared in the sky as a star. Please give it to me, and look up," Rajeswari spoke in jest.

She tore open and read the telegram. Kandan for a while stood watching the crowding fury of the waters as if they mirrored the deep tumult of his own heart and the struggle and the unrest of all life on land.

The telegram read:

RANGASWAMI, I.C.S.,
Tranquebar.

Transferred as Assistant Settlement Officer to Palni. Join forthwith.

Rajeswari Bai jumped for joy like a child.

"Kanda, there's already prophecy in my words. I foretold it to Rangan. I don't believe he would still think of going out as a Settlement Officer, measuring mountain slopes while he ought to be fighting for his Motherland. Rangan, as a friend, is a weak soul full of sophistry, rugged metaphors, and wild similes. As a fighter, British Raj will find in him a foeman worthy of its steel."

Kandan exclaimed in incredulous tones, "Impossible to believe this telegram! Rangan to be degraded into a Settlement Officer for no reason, and all on a sudden. Impossible, unless it be that a faithful report of all our conversation is being telegraphed to the Government of Madras every evening."

Ponnan stood impatiently digging the sand with his right toe and restlessly crushing his palm as if in respectful prayer for orders. He ventured to ask for Rangan respectfully, "Where's the Collector *dorai*, madam?"

"Ponna, there he is in the open turret—look aloft. Take this to him. But he is no more the Collector *dorai* though you may continue to call him so."

Rajeswari smiled rejoicingly. But Kandan asked seriously, when Ponnan had left: "Rajee, are you sure Ponnan is our faithful servant, and not a spy from Madras?"

"Kanda, you say you have since traced his relationship to you through your mother, some cousin, distant cousin."

"That does not save him from becoming a spy. Somehow I don't like his looks—there is a sly trickish twinkle in his eyes. We must watch him a little more carefully and keenly."

"His looks were worse, and he is improving quickly, changing under the magnetic spell of Sarasvati."

"At any rate, we must watch him a little more carefully."

"A very cousinly feeling!"

(5)

Ponnan quickly covered the level stretch of sand and was half way up to the fort. But he had another telegram in his pocket in code words. He must destroy it immediately. For the very good news it contained he wanted to read it once again before he destroyed it. So he took it out cautiously, and it ran as follows:

Promoted for excellent work, by fifty rupees. Continue watching movements send full report. If, as you say, Mr. Mudaliar too is likely to join, and Rangaswami dislikes the transfer and thinks of resigning, wire at once.

Though it was in code words Ponnan did not consider it safe to keep it himself. He saw the fresh-water well on the foreshore near the fort and no one drawing water for the moment. He tore the telegram to bits and sent them flying down the well.

He looked aloft and fancied that Rangan and Sarasvati had seen him in the act.

A bead of perspiration came rolling down his forehead and gathered into a little drop on his eyebrow. Ponnan hurried up the narrow flight of steps to deliver the other telegram to his master. But Ponnan while ascending the winding steps amidst the cracked domes had a strange thought about the fresh-water well so near the sea.

Why is the well so near the sea ever so full of fresh water? Is it like the thoughts and deeds of good men even when they are always surrounded by bad people?

Why is the sea ever so saltish even though hundreds of rivers pour their sweet, fresh waters into it every minute, day and night? Is it quite like himself?

But this reverie was broken by the sharp voice of Kamakshi who, emerging from the other side of a lofty dome, asked in a tone of reprimand, "Ponna, what did you throw into that drinking well? Something that would foul its water? Don't you know that this is the only fresh-water well in the whole fort?"

Ever since they met each other on the platform of the Akkur railway station, Ponnan was irresistably feeling drawn to Kamakshi, and already he had developed a great tenderness for her.

"What did I throw into the well? Nothing, sweet Kamakshi, nothing that would foul the fresh water or offend your taste. Shall I tell you—only if you won't be angry with me—shall I tell you, a love-letter that I dared not crush into your tender hands at some secret hour—so I threw it into the well that it might sweeten the water you drink and thus pour its love-laden song into your soul."

Ponnan drew audaciously from his imagination, but in the sentiment of love he so tenderly expressed towards Kamakshi, he was thoroughly sincere. Kamakshi had a bird-like beauty and charm all her own, somewhat heightened by the lonely looks of her lotus eyes, a little frosted by secret tears.

Kamakshi drooped her long-lashed eyelids and by way of breaking the embarrassment asked, "The telegram in hand, Ponna,—is it for the Collector *dorai*?"

"Yes, for the Collector, sweet Kamakshi. I'll run up like a squirrel, deliver it in a second and return—pray, wait a minute."

(6)

Ponnan had hardly disappeared from view. Kamakshi stood throbbing with fear at the audacious approach and the promised voluptuous return of

Ponnan whom she instinctively both liked and disliked from the very beginning.

Padma emerged from another corner of the vast and rugged terrace studded with cracked domes, and greeted Kamakshi with a tenderness which youth and sincerity alone can command, "Won't you tell me, Kamakshi, what that scoundrel, Ponnan, poured in whispers into your innocent ears? Be warned of him."

Kamakshi was startled but in a moment composed herself and looked at him with a sigh of relief and satisfaction.

"Ever since I met him at the Coleroon station," Padma continued feeling assured by her confidence in him which her looks signalled, "I've been doing nothing but watching him, spying him and his devious ways. Rangan trusts him implicitly. But I do really think he is a spy set up by the Government to watch the movements of Rangan and Rajeswari. He is a C. I. D., I think, Kamakshi—he has so far successfully fooled both Rangan and Rajee. Allow him not to ensnare you, my pretty, pretty bird, Kamakshi."

Kamakshi blushed heavily but with a pleasant smile deepening her charm. In Padma's lotus-face too there was a magnet-glow, the shine of intelligence of courageous seventeen. Kamakshi felt irresistably drawn to Padma.

"No, no, Padma, don't get unnecessarily alarmed on my account; though still young and innocent like you, years of adversity have taught me the ways of men and the wiles of this world. I've learnt to protect myself. The ugly cactus as well as the lovely rose grows its own thorns against the hour of peril."

A smile, as suggestive as a bud about to bloom, dimpled her cheeks. In that magic eddy, Padma lost his infant heart. He pulsed with love whose depths his being knew not but felt like the tremors of a distant earthquake. It was the first time that Padma was ever moved by a woman.

Kamakshi also for all her reliant plea of self-protection felt a strange revolution in her being, a flooding of the heart, a sense of pure and noble fulfilment that comes but once in her life to a woman.

Padma and Kamakshi spoke not another word for half-an-hour. But they both gazed on in wonder at the ceaseless tumult of the sea with a like tumult in their own hearts. Now and then in the guise of taking a flank view of the lovely landscape between the sea and the river, Padma and Kamakshi each took a fill of the other, and felt as unsatisfied as ever.

(7)

Meanwhile, Kandan and Rajeswari were speculating how Rangan would receive this news of transfer, whether he would view it at all as a mark of degradation.

"I rather think, Rajee, that Rangan won't easily give up the job, taking a sentimental view of things. You know that the I. C. S. is a little kingship, and its atmosphere knows not the common depression, stress and storm of our humble lives."

"Then, you say, Kanda, that he would give us up and join duty as a Settlement Officer and do penance on the Palni Hills to promote his patriotism! It's hard for me to believe it of Rangan, though I know he is not made of the heroic stuff of which men, like you, are made. But the third-class ticket adventure at Egmore has bitten into his soul. It's often trifles that derail a mighty mind in motion. Besides, Sarasvati is a new factor. She is a first-class patriot, a seer, a magnet-force, and an organising genius of the first order; and for aught I know she won't allow her gifted brother to bear the benumbing rule of red-tapes and flags. Nor will I, if I still count for anything at all in his eyes."

"Yes, Rajee, you are the decisive factor, I forgot all about it. Now I'm sure he will give up the job at once. Look up, Rajee, they are coming down in splendid haste full of meaning and freedom in their movements—and Ponnan is flying for life—what's the matter?"

Yes, Ponnan was running at top speed to the post-office near by with a sheet of paper in his hand.

"I'm sure, Kanda, he is telegraphing his resignation."

Rangan came running to the shore shouting like a child who has changed a cake for a toy: "I've, Rajee, kicked up the d—d thing by wire just now. Your words are indeed quite prophetic—Settlement Officer on Palni Hills! I fear that it's not Ponnan but you, the spy in the C. I. D., fully in the know of the secrets of this wonderful Government."

"Yes, yes, the secret to make heroes of civilians and patriots of magistrates," Rajee responded laughing.

Hardly these words had been uttered, when the stately Auburn Sedan came hooting and racing to the sea-shore, flying like a sea-bird over the spacious and beautiful *maidan* that lies to the north of the fort.

Chockalinga alighted first; then Sundaram and Karian humbly followed him.

"Collector *dorai*, I've come to beg a favour of you: to intercede on our behalf with the railway authorities at Tanjore. Karian and Sundaram, two of my friends, have been dismissed from service as a result of the collision for which I was alone responsible, by running the train before time. Pray, move in the matter, Collector *dorai*,—you will have my life-long gratitude."

"I'm no more the Collector, Mr. Mudaliar, no more than you. I have resigned the job at the call of the country. Leading *mirasdars*, like you, should help us at this critical hour when a new and a great India is being born." Rangan had already begun his special service to the country with his eloquent tongue.

"Yes, Mr. Mudaliar, you too should join us as the scion of an ancient house and as the natural leader of these men," Rajeswari spoke with moving sincerity.

Sarasvati spoke not but stood motionless yet vivid like an *ambal* in an ancient shrine. She seemed to turn on Mudaliar her calm collected eyes that were pools of tranquillity, as if in earnest spiritual entreaty for the cause of the great Mother. Chockalinga felt a throbbing change in the sacred *sandhya* hour of the setting sun.

The restless sea threw on the shore wave after wave of wondrous motion, shape, and beauty. Chockalinga stood speeechless at the sea-change that was coming over him silently but swiftly. Standing in the very midst of the spraying waters,—it was the true baptismal hour to him—the waves rolling from the far-off depths of the sea and breaking at his very feet in cooling showers, and the waves of light from the marvellous eyes of Sarasvati illumining him with a new vision of life.

CHAPTER XVII

WORDS AND DEEDS

(1)

"RANGA, it's a pity you still believe in the magic of words. Speech is fatal to action. You know it more than I do, both its pyschology and its ethics, but some mysterious force of your own native instinct is drawing you to the lure of words." Thus Kandan pleaded with a sincerity that was well-reflected in a suffused glow that spread over his face. This impassioned appeal relieved his aching heart.

Kandan and Sarasvati, Rangan and Rajeswari were seated in a circle on the first terrace of the fort. The breeze was blowing in steadily and the setting sun threw a flood of golden light on the trembling waves, which gallopped to the shore one after the other as if in a race to catch first the glory of the sinking sun.

"No, no, Kanda, you still hold to your Oxford views. You despise the glory of words, though oftentimes I've envied your own quiet verbal charm and dignity. Words too have a high place in the scheme of life. Where action fails words have often won—you can cut a knot with a sword, but stitch you can't do with a sword but need a needle, and you have to ply it unceasingly in a series of endless minor strokes. But for the glory of words, Kanda, the whole history of our race would have been a very different thing—mere clod of earth untouched by fire ; a mere waste-land, dry and dreary, with no flower garden therein. It may be that words, like fire, are double-edged. You may destroy as well as build beautifully; build with words the finest edifice to the spirit of man, as great and lasting as the pyramids. It's just the one gift which tells off the man from the beast—words, words."

"Speak like gods and act like beasts, that is the first weakness of man, Ranga. I must dissent from this extreme eulogy of the tongue. The most beautiful words and the choicest phrases have never won the freedom of a nation, not even cured its own slave-mind. *Yoga* is disciplined action. India has preached since the *Vedic* days the loftiest ideals, perfect as the Himalayan peaks, and left them there unrealised in deeds. In action, we are nowhere. That is why our life is so uneven, and we so low and poor among the nations ; stagnant, shallow pools, at different levels, what should have flowed into a glorious, fertilising river fed by eternal snows."

"Kanda, this speech itself from you tells me of the highest action-value of words ; it stirs me."

"What are we worth, Ranga, without deeds which alone have the power of cleansing the channels of life, converting into bliss the wild energy of words? Words are but symbols of a moving spirit, a fire glowing within. They are rather like the sparks that fly in the air, for a fleeting second only to die. They illumine nothing but the darkness around; they warm nothing. Perhaps they tell you that the flame is still unsteady and needs more of nursing care to keep it alive."

Kandan shook his head decidedly as if all doubts were at rest, at least for him, and continued, "Action is the soul of life, Ranga. Words are but sparks which die peacefully in silence the moment the flame of action has got steady. Let us act, Ranga. Let us put our dreams into action and realise them. Without honest, untiring, selfless work, there is no happiness for our long-ailing land; wise but weak because we have not got the courage for action to do selfless work. To keep a nation great and alive at least ten per cent must always be prepared to die in action for an unknown, selfless cause."

"Words may be sparks, Kanda, but they are divine sparks, like the broken light from the stars. Words themselves are pure action at its highest, Kanda. Even at the lowest, they are the loyal first steps to action. You can't run a ladder without rungs, and a political ladder at that—unless of course you are a first-class *yogi*. For mass action nothing like words. The intricate executive mechanism of man refuses to work unless it be well-oiled by words. Without words, the only medium of exchange of ideas, so dear to man, what can you do? You may as well draw water from yonder well on the shore without a rope or a bucket! I'm less ambitious."

"Ranga, it's your figures of speech that deny you the true taste of life. They are really taking you away far, far from a true sense of values, the nature of reality."

"Kanda, I know that you distrust them but they illumine me with flashes of light along the darkest corridors; make me see things better. Action isolates life, breaks it up into little stagnant pools of water amidst rocks and holes, shrubs and jungles. Words are liquid in their action; they spread and move like monsoon rains making rivers, fertilising the high and the low, and carry a sacred, even gift to all. Pray don't underrate the value of words; then you underrate your very self. Our own Congress knew it so well for thirty years and it is now the greatest monument to the glory of words. In a great national movement like ours, nothing like words. When a mighty lake is chafing its bunds, do you go on baling its restless waters with rope and bucket; simply open out a surplus weir of safety and sacrifice. Pray, don't oppose me in this, Kanda. We must begin the movement in the District by calling a big meeting; words alone will stir these refined, decadent people. Tell them of their great past and make a sentimental appeal which would rouse them."

"You would be simply courting trouble without succeeding in doing anything. Who cares for speeches in these days? Only work counts," Kandan replied calmly.

"Kanda, politics are not like work in the laboratory where you may toil quietly and laboriously for years and announce the result of your researches some day to a wondering world in ten words like Einstein and profit the whole race by it. The laboratory of man, the political animal, is out in the open. Every street corner is his. Words alone can kindle and set free the frozen heart and thaw it to a magic flow of feelings. And when the time comes to harness this flow to the wheel of action, action comes easily in its own wake, like thunder after lightning. For both are twins, Kanda. Please don't oppose the holding of a big meeting to stir this pond of our District. To dredge the slime you have to stir the muddy water. We'll hold it on this very beautiful *maidan* which seems to have been waiting these peaceful years only for some such glorious, active end. Let us declare war from here so that the whole world may hear us."

"How do you get publicity for your meeting—by beat of tom-tom?"

"Beat of tom-tom! Quite primitive, Kanda; why, I'll wire the news to the Madras papers and ask the editors to grind a leading note; all of them are my friends and they will rejoice in my resignation and sacrifice. They will feature the news."

"Now I understand why you want a meeting, Ranga, that you may make some news of your resignation and get a leader for your sacrifice." Rajee pricked the bubble, and Rangan seemed to enjoy the hit without any sacrifice of words this time.

"Rajee, you may mock at me and my patriotism. But nothing like a meeting to strike the imagination of the rustic folk and rouse the patriotic feelings of the people. It pours courage into the quaking heart; crowd psychology creates a kind of courage, a new vision of life. In a great national movement like ours which has to cover the whole of a sub-continent, nothing like the spreading glory of words. Rajee, words and deeds are one. That is the highest concept. They are twins; not step-brothers by different mothers as you conceive them to be,—a false philosophy of life."

Everyone seemed to listen to Rangan intently, and encouraged by this silence Rangan began to hammer while the iron was still hot. "Dear Kanda, pray don't oppose the holding of a meeting. We'll hold it on this beautiful *maidan*. I'll wire the news to the Madras papers. In flaming headlines Tranquebar will appear, and this old, mouldy town of the eighteenth century will throb with the pulse of renascent India. Kanda, if you are still unconvinced by my words, ask Rajee. I think that she too is of my way of thinking and I trust her words on critical occasions."

Rajee said in a very serious voice: "Kanda, I bow to your judgment though I agree with Rangan to a limited extent. Let us hold but one meeting to tell the whole world of the grand change that has come over Rangan and the great District of his birth—just half-an-hour for the flow of his feelings and the magic craft of his oratory. Let Rangan blow off the steam so that he may settle down to work the better. Where is the orator born who cares to go perchance to jail even without one farewell speech or message to his fellow countrymen? Pray, Kanda, don't ask human nature to perform the impossible."

"But, Ranga, you are opposed by your own sister who pleads for some quiet work as an example to all. She says, words have only misled men. Who can neglect her wise words?" Kandan asked.

"Kanda, dearly I love my sister. But what does she know of the world and the subtle ways of high politics? She has no doubt a wonderful intuition and almost a second sight into men and things. But in these minor, mundane matters her lofty mind does not even touch the ground. Why should it? Monsoon clouds, to fill a lake with fresh water, do they bend and bow or circle around the bed of a lake? They roam in the spacious sky, and rain from lofty heights and scatter wild and plenty the beautiful drops of rain, like Kubera his riches. The rolling drops roll a little more and form a precious rivulet till they seek a place of safety which we call a lake."

Sarasvati quickly replied before the silver voice of Rangan had quite finished its rhythmic peals of music: "I'm no match, indeed, to my brother's gifts of oratory. He plays with figures of speech like those urchins there picking shells on the shore and pelting the mighty waves of the sea. What does it matter to them that they raise no ripples on the waves or in the sea? Sport is sport, and life is one grand *leela*, as seers say. Yes, as Rajee says, Rangan may be allowed the last chance for his oratory—I've not heard him till now—ere he goes to jail like a true patriot. But my only fear is that the meeting itself may be prohibited by the police and the Collector."

"Well said, Sarasvati, that's also my fear and hope. Quite like you—there's a prophetic ring in your speech," Kandan cried with admiration in his eyes.

But Rangan, rushed a torrent of words: "Never, never, impossible. Mr. Lance is not a fool to play with me. It was but yesterday I was the Collector's right hand, and my friend, Nataraja, who is still there in my place, won't allow dealing with me so lightly. If only to prove my words and show my strength, we should hold a meeting."

Chockalinga, who felt that his prestige too was involved in this matter, broke his long and reverent silence and said: "No, no, the Collector knows that I too have joined hands with you, and they won't break up or prohibit the meeting. I stand guarantee for that. Yes, let us hold the meeting and see. I'll bring the whole Taluk into this sacred square."

Chockalinga underwent the change that an eddy feels when it resolves back again into the calm, flowing water after the whirling force of passion has spent itself.

It was decided eventually that a meeting should be held and Chockalinga spoke in a voice of final decision: "I'll drive the whole Taluk into this sacred square on Friday evening at four. I'll fill Tranquebar and this fort with my Nandan, Mookkan, and Katteri; with my Irullan, Karuppan, and Irullappan; Govindan, Pavadai, and Nallan. Nochi will lead the clan. They are brave and loyal fellows, the like of whom you can never see. I place entirely at your disposal, all my men."

Meanwhile, Rangan scribbled a few lines on a note paper and called out, "Ponna, where are you? Take this out to the post-office and telegraph it at once."

Of course Ponnan was ever ready. He was standing near by. He briskly executed the order.

"Is that a telegram to the Madras papers?"

"Yes," came the laconic reply from Rangan.

Rangan began to feel the strength of an elephant. He vowed to work in silence. After all words are words, and deeds are deeds.

(2)

At about the same time, a couple of days later, another scene of the same drama was being enacted at Vallam, the official residence of the Collector of Tanjore. Vallam is a little village beautifully situated on the dry, bracing uplands of Tanjore, enjoying the rich products of the Cauvery Delta and claiming at the same time immunity from its humid and enervating climate.

The District of Tanjore, in fertility, population, wealth, refinement, and ancient traditions, is one of the foremost in South India and its Collectorship is the current equivalent to the old kingship of the Cholas. It is the most coveted prize in the Indian Civil Service of the Tamil Land.

Mr. Lance had taken twenty-three years to ripen into the Collector of Tanjore. He was a man of deeds, not of words. But he always thought that for his powers, both mental and moral, even a Collectorship had become too opaque and narrow a bushel. For a wiser decision while young he should have ended to his heart's content, laying at the service of the Empire a career as brilliant as Lord Cromer's in Egypt or Marshall Lyuatey's in Morroco, nay even of Lord Curzon in India. So

Mr. Lance had to be content with the highest rung in the ladder of his own early choice, and too long a stay even in the highest rung not only curtails ambition and energy but the higher and the more difficult quality of sympathy. Mr. Lance was discontented with himself.

Mr. Lance had a paternal notion of the welfare of the people committed to his charge, the notion generated in the dry traditions of his great service. He had by nature a heart for the poor and almost a Martian fondness for straight irrigation channels, though he knew as a student of dynamics that water-drops, like human footsteps, delight to take a winding course. For, he believed in the first duty of the governing mind that wayward freedom either of water-drop or of man must be controlled and regulated at all cost.

When he first heard that the quiet of his District was likely to be disturbed by the freedom craze that was blowing like a tempest all over the country, he had decided on prompt measures. He summoned a conference of the big three of the district ; the District Superintendent of Police and the Assistant Collector who was supposed to be his chief adviser, and himself.

" Mr. Lance, you do your own inherent goodness and turn for statesmanship much wrong. Nothing can disturb the chronic quiet of my own District, even if Gandhiji shifts his headquarters from Sabarmati to Tanjore. I'm born and bred in this

District, I know the temper of my people. Nothing will move them to war. I know their pulse ; there's no danger now. No trouble, Mr. Lance, in my District, unless you load them with repression and turn the sheep to fight. My District once produced pioneers and statesmen but now it produces only able vakil *gumasthas*, petition-writers, canvassing agents and accountants."

"And every now and then a brilliant Assistant Collector."

Mr. Natarajan, the Assistant Collector, gracefully accepted the compliment and said affably, "I repeat, Mr. Lance, don't make any fuss about this Tranquebar affair. It will die an inane death after a few speeches from Rangan. Of all places on earth, Tranquebar! Tranquebar,—old, dilapidated, with nothing but salt-eaten ruins—not even crabs thrive there!"

"But, Nataraja, I'm afraid of Kandan—it was you who made me fear him. You know him better—that was why I left him undisturbed till now, though our valued friend, Mr. Mudaliar, wanted to book him."

"Yes, I know Kandan quite well. He is a good and sincere worker. He may touch and improve a few men or villages here and there, but he has not that blazing power to rouse to action on a grand scale a large body of men. He is not an advertiser, and without it no work, not even patriotic selfless work, can ever spread. Even a saint can't work magic under modern conditions without publicity."

"But now that Rangan has also joined Kandan, the materials for an explosion are ready according to your own rules of reckoning—and we must prevent their coming together; it is commonsense; is it not, Nataraja?"

"I know the whole brood—I lived with them three years at Oxford and I know Rajeswari Bai as well. She has a strange power of drawing men towards her Now that Rangan has resigned, I hope my transfer to Guntur stands cancelled?"

"You don't like to face that work at Guntur?"

"I should rather not, unless duty makes it inevitable for me. Your whole policy is wrong, and you are wholly underrating the forces of the strong love of freedom that is stirring and making New India. Kindness will win you many friends all over and benefit you in the long run. Send out a Viceroy like MacDonald, or better, manage to get one Mac for each District, one who can lisp mystic words of international fellowship, the Indian problem is solved for the present. MacDonald is a clever Scot."

"You know him personally, Nataraja?"

"Yes, very well; why, all of us, especially Rangan who had also worked for him in general elections; and Rangan too can command beautifully those vague words of sympathy; but Kandan, who also knows him, does not trust him at all as he thinks that the cause of Labour will never be safe in his hands, especially Labour in power. He thinks of him as too much of a sentimental individualist. He can work hard in opposition in the formative periods of a great humanitarian movement, but can't lead a party to victory while in power, minting words into deeds with sovereign courage, but will forsake it undoubtedly in its critical hour on some convenient ground of conscience or principle."

"Nataraja, let us leave imperial problems to the Prime Minister. My District troubles are enough for me now. But from what you say, I fear all the more this combination of Rangan, Kandan, and Rajeswari at Tranquebar. Such people can make even kings of crabs. I trust your prudent head generally, but in this matter you are underestimating the joint effect. We must take energetic steps lest the peace of the District be disturbed. The young Mudaliar, if he be won over,—his influence there will lead to serious trouble. He has a tremendous following in his Taluk and his fellows are dare-devils who would cheerfully leap into fire for the sake of their master."

"That may make matters different, Mr. Lance, I agree. But Mr. Mudaliar has nothing to gain from that alliance; on the other hand he would lose all his splendid fortune. I think he is a safe fellow; he has no patriotic touch, and his love of elections to the local bodies is more for the sake of fine roads for his Auburn car. His conversion is an impossibility, Mr. Lance—for aught I know of human nature!"

"But, Nataraja, you forget your own words—all the three there have got rare magnetic power over men. That's just also what the Government report from Madras tells me."

"Yes, that is why I say once again, don't launch on repression now and give them a chance to exercise their witchcraft. Rangan when aggrieved is no doubt a real power. He has such a mastery of emotional oratory that his eloquence touches the marrow of one's bones. Let us get accurate news and see. What does our Superintendent say?"

"What do you say, D. S. P.?" the Collector asked.

"I must be plain and frank. I won't be responsible for the peace of the place, sir, unless some immediate steps are taken to prevent the meeting which is sure to end in a bloody riot. The leaders should be bound over or clapped in jail for at least three months. They should not be allowed to go about stirring villages with new and strange ideas. Even a year ago I reported that Kandan should be made to cease his activities."

"What is the latest news?"

"We'll have it in ten minutes." The D. S. P. replied straining his eyes as if expecting some arrival.

Yes, in ten minutes a messenger came running with a telegram in hand.

"Yes, everything is taking place as I predicted. Here is the latest news: 'All tending towards a conflagration. Even Mr. Mudaliar has definitely joined the movement. A public meeting on the biggest scale to be held on Friday evening at four. Breaches of the peace certain, unless the meeting is prohibited. Even Ponnan, C.I.D.'s loyalty doubtful; he seems to have joined them; at any rate it is not certain on which side he is.'"

The D. S. P. paused for a moment wiping the excited sweat on his brow and said, "This is the report from one of the ablest and most reliable of my men. My duty is plain, sir. If Mr. Mudaliar has joined the movement, the local Police won't fire a shot. We must use the Malabar reserves. We must send there a strong contingent immediately, and take charge of the fort which is still in their hands. By wire they must be asked to quit." The D. S. P. was strong and decided.

"I agree with you. There's no good in being slow in these vital matters. You Tamils, Nataraja, have a proverb: 'What is the use of clutching at the tail after failing to catch by the horns'—only kicks. Yes, 'a stitch in time saves nine,' as the D. S. P. wisely reminds me of our own proverb. Well, I give you orders to make adequate police arrangements but don't precipitate matters by any rash deed. I shall also camp very near at Akkur on Friday morning and watch developments."

Again another peon came running with another message. "'The meeting is elaborately advertised, the countryside is aflame with enthusiasm Rangan and Rajeswari are terribly active. Messages by wire have been sent to all the Madras papers—and also a message to A. P. I. with a friendly request to Reuter to flash a line abroad. Rangan and Rajeswari are the moving spirits; and a young boy by name Padma, and a girl by name Kamakshi are doing the work of ten; they are all visiting one village after another, lecturing and doing *bhajanu* and promising the poor tax-free one acre holdings. All revolution and socialism inflaming agrarian discontent. Trouble is certain on Friday, as sure as sunrise.'"

Mr. Lance was perturbed. He thought and mused and stroked his fingers on his right thigh, as if that would yield some message to the brain and clear the line of decision. It was a reverie stroke. Would he become even more famous than Cromer or Curzon? He abruptly dismissed Natarajan and the D. S. P., and retired to his drawing-room to think clearly of the great problem of a disturbed district for the first time in his long career of twenty-three years of peace and plenty.

(3)

When Mr. Lance, the Collector was puzzled about the peace of his district, Raghu, the humble clerk in the Taluq Office at Shiyali, was equally perplexed about the peace and certainty of his official tenure. For Raghu had reached in the last week a crisis in his own conscience and office-work. Padma's revolt had made him introspective, and later the new Tahsildar thoroughly provoking. Instead of the promised inspection by the Deputy Collector, which did not come off, there was a change of Tahsildar at the Shiyali Taluq Office at the last moment. The ambitious graduate Raghu who had specialised in economics and labour problems for the benefit of the public had to apply his specialised knowledge remorselessly to his own personal affairs.

Neelakshi sat as usual on the pial of her house, but bandied words no more with the passer-by or invited the lazy to a gossip. She silently watched the street-ends straining her eyes in anxiety. Every boy coming at a distance seemed to her to bear a hopeful resemblance to Padma—a constant mirage-like deception crushed her virile spirit and benumbed her energy. The loss of Padma, her youngest, was too much for her to bear, proud and self-contained though she had always been even in severe adversity. Yet, is not hope in the maternal bosom perennial? Neelakshi continued to gaze on the stream of street-traffic day by day—and footsteps that rushed along the streets in the dark of the night reminded her of Padma's characteristic impatient rush. And every night found and left her sleepless.

Even Chandru deserted her. He did not care to hold his slate that threatening way for Neelakshi responded not: she had become utterly listless and immobile. So, Chandru had joined the boys and girls in the street to play with. And Neela had not the spirits to chide the boy as she would in normal times.

On this fateful evening as well, Neelakshi sat, sad and wistful, growing more and more prayerful at heart.

The temple bells were pealing the glory of God in clear tones calling the lay and the pious to the worship of the matin hour. Neela, not over-religious by temperament, remembered her Maker in mute worship in her hour of trial. She prayed for the early return of Padma. And Raghu came trotting along in unusual mirth, clearing at one bound the flight of steps to his house, like a colt not harnessed to work for many a day. Neela received him with open arms judging that there must be surely glad tidings for so much joy—probably Padma had been discovered.

"Raghu, it gladdens me to see you so merry as of old—has Padma been found?"

"Has Padma been found! Mother, do you still dream of Padma's return. He must be now somewhere near Haridwar or Benares. You'll hear of him not now, but some years hence—patiently wait for that happy day—Padma is a brave and upright boy; he will bring nothing but honour to our family." Raghu spoke with a calm joy in his face.

"Then, Raghu, what makes you so happy?"

"Mother, I am to-day a free man; now that Padma is lost to the country's cause, I'll, his elder brother, step into his place and do public work from now: work for the uplift of India."

"What are you talking, Raghu? Are you mad or drunk?"

"Yes, mother, drunk with the wine of freedom. No more am I a slave at the desk grinding accounts for an alien rule to keep a pampered system going. I'm no more a slave. My resignation has been accepted readily on the spot by the new Tahsildar himself."

"What Raghu—what a mad act in a foolish hour—without consulting me!" Neela could not believe her own ears. "Are you joking or speaking the truth?"

"Truth—nothing but the truth, mother. Are you not proud of me to-day that I've won my freedom so that I may work for the public cause. Mother, the thing is in the air—who can escape it? I now understand Padma and his patriotic, truant ways."

"But, Raghu—we are not *sanyasins*—"

"Think not of the morrow, mother; He who has planted the tree will water it, as the ancient Tamil proverb goes. God will feed all mouths—look at yonder sparrow chirping in freedom-flights—does it think of the morrow?"

Without another word and without pausing for his mother's reply, Raghu went into the house, threw carelessly his soiled cap and dust-laden coat on a bench weighted with paddy bags on which squirrels played picking the grains one by one running to and fro.

Raghu, exclaiming, "Mother, look at these happy squirrels; draw a lesson from them, and plan our lives," marched off to the Uppanar river like a schoolboy on the eve of the summer vacation. He roamed at large on fields and banks for three hours and more, and returned home late at night at 9 o'clock. Neelakshi was sitting as usual on the pial anxiously awaiting the return of Raghu and perchance of Padma. The moon poured her bright light pensively on the streets.

"Raghu, I can't understand you—you are behaving more wildly than Padma or Chandru!"

Had Chandru heard this indictment of him he would have come threatening his grandmother with his slate which he had since supplemented with a vigorous stick. But Chandru was fast asleep.

Raghu's temper rose a little at his mother's angry words. But he controlled it and said: "Mother, don't go on accusing me at random when I am enjoying the hour of freedom. I'm going to put my doctrines to practice. Why did you educate me at so much cost and sacrifice? For my fallen country, I've sketched a ten-year plan of progress on a grand, grand socialistic base, where each shall give to society his best, and each shall get in return what he needs for the day on the simple rule of plain living and high thinking—have you heard the latest news, mother? It's stirring the whole district into a commotion."

Neelakshi was in a state of impassive calm. Raghu seeing her quite unmoved by his grandiose plan which had failed to provoke from his mother even the usual alert critical retort, continued in a subdued voice: "Mother, aren't you following me at all! Haven't you heard the latest news? Even Shiyali is excited over it. At Tranquebar they are holding the biggest meeting that ever took place in our land since the days of Karikalan. To organise and lead it, a Collector, a patriotic young Tamil, Rangan by name, has resigned his job, and a lady has come all the way from Bombay, the only daughter of a millionaire, sacrificing all for the cause of her country's freedom."

Raghu paused a moment and leisurely surveyed his home and said in a voice of rising confidence: "I am going to join straightaway Rangan and Rajeswari and help the country's cause. Mother, I'll storm the platform, and preach my ten-year plan of work to the vast multitude assembled there and convert the leaders to my creed. The Tamil land will soon echo with a new name, my name. Aren't you proud, mother? At last, at last I am finding a mode of expression for myself, and now I can use something of what I have learnt at college at so much of your sacrifice, dear mother."

"Raghu, you are in a state of wild frenzy; I suspect your sanity," Neelakshi slowly replied recollecting herself and asserting her dignity. "Raghu, I'm unable to follow you—mere words, words, words, unrelated to your real life. It'll land you in chaos and ruin your home and kill your mother. Are you also going to desert me like Padma in my old days—they have taught well filial duty at college—no doubt *kaliyuga* is fast ripening and the ancient prophecy is coming true;—anarchy is ahead; it's spreading fast like a forest fire, from nation to school, from school to home. Raghu, you want me to live or die?" And she added after a pause for breath: "Your foolish action, Raghu, is like breaking the churn in despair when you are about to gather the cream of your hard work for years, alas!"

"I want you not to die, mother! I want you to live long, to live the longest, to live till you see me achieve success to your heart's content, and bring swaraj to our aching motherland."

Raghu poured his words in an emphatic voice, and paused a moment as if gathering his wide-spread thoughts into a special and happy focus. "Perchance, mother, at Tranquebar our Padma may, if he happen to be roaming still near by—surely he will, attend the meeting, the biggest thing in promise that has so far been planned or attempted in our Tamil land. If I meet him I'll surely bring him to you for a day at least before we both start again on public work. Mother, to be true to my education on which you have lavished your dearest love and sacrifices, I should do something for the freedom-fight and the commonweal of the land which is as sacred to me, mother, as yourself, and so we call it the motherland."

"And we and our home?" asked Neelakshi in speechless rage.

"As for you and our home, mother, sell my wife's jewels; alas, that I've not put by anything—how could I have saved anything on thirty rupees a month. Her jewels will surely last you for two years—and our struggle at the worst will not be at a stretch for more than two years. Then let us see. I feel the call, mother, earnestly—it seems Padma has left his political ghost to stir me to action."

Raghu paused a moment in reflection and added: "If you don't like this, pray send my wife and my boy to her father's place, and you yourself go to my eldest brother at Madura. Forget the old quarrel a dozen years ago with your daughter-in-law—he will treat you royally. He has long been inviting you."

Neelakshi was about to speak a word in scorn and move off, but Raghu quickly signed to her to be calm and spoke: "Mother, stay a moment longer—have an eye on Chandru, my boy; I may not be here to see him grow from lisp to lisp, but tell him now and then when he calls for me, that his father has gone on duty's call, to make at least the life of the younger generation better, and wipe out an ancient reproach to this sacred land. You have endured many trials in your long life, mother? Why not this little surrender of your son, one of seven, at the united call of the nation!"

"Never, never, Raghu, unless you want me to die? So long as I am alive you shall never leave my home without my permission or go against my wishes. A frail, drudging clerk like you, Raghu, is already broken up with misfortune and over-work. What service and sacrifice can you do to the country against the might of the British Raj. You will simply swell the problem of providing the feed for so many public workers or the crowd in the jails if you have the courage to get in." Neela with her innate love of command tried to assert herself as a last chance against this first open revolt of her boy which she could never really understand. So she threw the harpoon in vile onslaught.

Raghu spoke not a word in reply to this mocking charge from his own mother but simply moved away from her towards the smoking kerosene lamp. He snatched a copy of the Bhagavad-Gita from a heap of out-worn books by his side, and began reading it by the pale lamp light. He became thoroughly absorbed in it in a moment.

Neelakshi changed the mode of her attack and began to conciliate her boy and convince him by the soft word that turneth away wrath. But Raghu spoke not a word or breathed even a sigh in reply but kept on reading the Gita intently. He had made up his mind for the patriotic dedication.

Neelakshi silently watched the absorbed concentration of her son till twelve o'clock midnight. Weary of lonely watch, defeated of purpose, and oppressed by the consciousness of a tragic future, Neela was overcome with sleep even while sitting. And soon she automatically fell asleep on the floor.

A few yards away Chandru slept rolling on his bed, now and then lisping a call for his father, and stretching out his sleeping hands in an empty embrace. Raghu, who was near by, tucked in a soothing pillow and returned to the Gita.

It was three o'clock very early dawn and an extreme stillness was in the air. Raghu laid down for a while his Gita and surveyed the scene of wreckage. His mother was fast asleep on the floor with a virile but thwarted expression of beauty still cleaving to her lips. His wife lay in a pathetic bundle very near the threshold of the kitchen—the very picture of a docile and charming Hindu wife. And Chandru was asleep near by, his tender feet projecting like lotus-buds amidst cotton sheets folded over him.

Raghu stood up. The first early train to Tranquebar was at four o'clock in the morning. He picked up the Gita; gently prostrated himself before his sleeping mother; kissed the lotus-feet of his darling Chandru who turned a little threateningly with a sudden start at the warm kisses showered, but fell back to deep sleep in the early morning hour patted on the back by his father.

Raghu once again prostrated himself before his mother as if asking silently for her forgiveness and blessing, dropped a gentle kiss on the forehead of his darling Chandru, stole a glance of farewell of his sleeping wife, seized the Gita tightly in his hand, drew back the bolt of the front-door without any noise, and leapt out softly like a cat in search of cheese.

Raghu reached the railway station just in time to see the searchlight of the train to Tranquebar, that played steadily on the arching track even from miles ahead.

CHAPTER XVIII

A LOG OF WOOD

(1)

It was very early dawn. The morning air was keen and dry. The twilight was just vanishing in the eastern sky. Venus, as the bright morning star, was paling before the spreading glory of the rising sun. The day was Friday, sacred to Venus and all auspicious work on earth. There was a pinching joy in the flooding sunshine of early morn.

Kandan was a very early riser like all those who sleep out in the open. He had just finished unusually all alone his morning walk. He was resting for a while on the bar of sand at the mouth of the river Veerasholan, enjoying in child-like wonder the charms of solitude and the calm that reigned over the sea and the river.

Kandan involuntarily dug the shore with his fingers till the spring water came oozing. He joyed in liberating the liquid life from the heavy choking sand that kept the waterdrop a prisoner in the underworld. He felt in that simple act of the child, victorious glee as if he had won Swaraj for India and watched with wonder and joy the oozing water bubbling into life and shape.

Kandan was lost in a *yogic* reverie: all life is alike. And a mighty wave came churning a roll of sand to his feet. From land to sea what a contrast and a wonder, he thought. On land the water is the prisoner and in the sea the land is the imprisoned. What seems is not the reality. There is something higher. That is the knotted problem of life. Consciousness is everything: its range and quality decide the grade of life. Action based on knowledge alone really counts, helps to realisation, guides the frail vessel of man to the other shore across uncharted seas.

Kandan continued in the same contemplative mood and picked up slowly one by one the broken as well as the full shells around him, and scratched therein with his fingernail some mystic letters of thought, and flung them one by one into the sea.

The sunshine came flooding everywhere and the morning calm was broken. The waves came sweeping on the shore in one huge tide singing the glory of the morning sun. The sea surged into the river and set the current going up. Kandan sat on a huge log of wood that lay nearby at the mouth of the river. It was some giant of the Ceylon forest, head cut off and bark peeled, now running its new career on the Coromandel coast, waiting to be shaped by the axe and the chisel of the carpenter into a catamaran to take merrily its daily dexterous business-trip in perilous seas.

The rushing water quickly volumed in strength in the river, and ate more and more of the shore coming nearer and nearer to where the log of wood lay like a dethroned king. In five minutes, this mighty and seemingly static log too would come under the sway of the sea. The whirling rush of salt water came endlessly in ever-widening circles of foam and tumult raging up the river.

Kandan stood up to avoid a morning drench and moved a little aside to watch the scene of slow but dramatic conquest. The waves broke into strong ripples in the river, till at last one big rush of water caught the thinner end of the log. It rolled the giant a little, showering water all over. A little shaken, it sat only the deeper in wet sand. Another sweep of water came and did likewise. Still the huge log lay unmoved like a beheaded giant.

Kandan thought and asked himself: "Why not I give the log a gentle push just at the proper moment when the rushing water rolls and lifts it a little?"

Kandan had to wait but a minute to act up to his wish. Another wave came spreading its charm round the log, and Kandan just at the right moment risking a morning splash of sea water gave it a firm push. The heavier end turned its big nose towards the stream, and galloped like a riding prince of old to a *svayamvara.* Another mighty wave came rushing along the river, and the ducal prince floated merrily into the mid-stream. It went up the river basking and glittering in the morning sun.

Kandan stood in wonder, lost in the stately motion of a thing that seemed but a while ago the most ponderous and safest thing in the world. He never took off his eyes from the drifting log of wood which sailed like a royal yacht. Indeed its touch was sovereign as it dipped and rose gaily in the rippling water.

A wondrous philosophy of life came in a flood to Kandan's mind. Kandan, standing on the sand-dunes and watching this river-scene was lost once again in a *yogic* reverie.

Are the poor, dumb, suffering, helpless unmoving masses of a nation like this log of wood—inert and dull to all appearance, till the fateful hour for swift motion comes when the flood of nationalism touches them? Then how quick and wondrous they float along the current with a sovereign air of gaiety, as if born to water and waiting for it these years like a Spanish galleon!

Just at that moment, Rangan and Rajeswari, Sarasvati and Kamakshi, and Chockalinga and Padma came running like children, and joined Kandan who was standing on the top of a sand-dune looking like a preacher about to begin his sermon, just waiting for his flock to gather.

(2)

"Did you push that log of wood into the river, Kanda?" asked Sarasvati in a voice of perfect calm and certainty.

"Yes, I did, Sarasvati, but how do you know it, unless you have seen it actually from some hiding-place!" Kandan exclaimed directing his wondering eyes on her.

"I, from some hiding place in this vast open of the sea and the shore! Why, Kanda, from the lingering look of love that you are sending trailing in its foaming wake—is the log of wood, teaching you also a lesson, something of the loftier thoughts and ways of life?" Sarasvati again asked with a smile of calm assurance.

Sarasvati continued before Kandan could answer, addressing Rajee: "Yes, Kandan takes his lessons and directions from these chance floating things which give the call to his inner voice to open out and speak. That is the way of all *advaitic* minds. To them the whole universe is beaming with a cosmic intelligence, and a floating straw can whisper to them the rise and fall of empires; and he who knows the script can read, even a child, the song in a blade of grass or a dewdrop!"

"Don't make me ridiculous, Sarasvati, in your own matchless way by exaggerating my oddities. Minds, which don't wholly work through reason like Rajee's and Rangan's, have got to kneel in worship before these random shafts of light from Heaven."

"No, no, Kanda, I think Sarasvati was seriously expounding you as well as herself, making an honest attempt to understand and interpret what I consider to be the higher consciousness in life. Sarasvati and you have given me a new vision," Rajee said devoutly.

"Well then, let us not forget the allegory of the log of wood, in the fine exchange of compliments. What did it tell you, Kanda—some parallel philosophy that would apply to immediate politics, if not to Rangan's meeting this evening." Sarasvati turned the flow of the conversation into its true bed.

"Well, then, you are right, this log of wood has a lesson for us all. At break of dawn, I found it as we have always found it these days since our arrival, buried in deep sand, safe and secure. When I sat on it this morning, I thought it was as safe as solid earth. The waves came rushing up the river, mad with the ecstasy of the full moon. In five minutes, this whilom king of the forest trembled at the touch of the dashing waves. Once, twice, thrice they came, making it more and more insecure. But still the log, though it rolled a little, like a giant in disturbed sleep, held firm to the ground; I thought the waves were powerless unless the whole sea came to their aid. I was impatient like a schoolboy and my hands craved for service. Why should I not render the waves some little human help? I just gave the log a gentle push at the just moment, and it is floating now merrily up the river. Perhaps even without my push it would have been carried into the river, sooner or later—"

"I'm not so sure of that, Kanda. It's quite possible that the flowing tide might have ebbed and the log remained there as safe as ever," Sarasvati dissented.

"May be, may be," Kandan agreed.

"But what is the lesson you draw therefrom, Kanda?" Rajee asked still eager to solve the puzzle.

"Why, Rajee, Kandan thinks that the log of wood stands for the masses; the waves rushing up the river is the tide of nationalism that is now sweeping the country, and the gentle push is the push of the patriot." Sarasvati solved the problem quietly.

"And Rangan's meeting this evening—is it the sea or the wave or the gentle push?" Rajee asked in a very serious tone which was greeted with peals of laughter in which Mr. Mudaliar too joined for courtesy's sake, though he did not quite catch the full trend of the philosophic discussion.

"Don't laugh at my meeting by propounding a metaphysical dilemma, Rajee. My meeting, if you please, is the gentle push as well as the raging sea. In its mighty current, you will soon see that it carries a whole forest of timber, a nation down the stream. Wait and see—what a splendid success the meeting is going to be!"

"Rangan's speech reminds me of the strange dream I had yesternight, Sarasvati—Rangan knows and envies me for my dreamless sleep. But the terrible dream I had in the small hours of this morning, unnerves me even now to repeat it—"

"Yes, Kandan sleeps like a child." Rangan endorsed.

(3)

"What is the dream, Kandà? Did you dream of Rangan's meeting—these dreams tell us sometimes wonderfully of the coming future—," Sarasvati asked Kandan with a note of eagerness and anxiety.

"That it ended in chaos or was broken up by the police?" Rajee asked with a sly smile.

"Rangan himself might have dreamt like that!" Sarasvati added her tribute of commentary to her brother's courage.

"Yes, surely he would have dreamt like that, but he could not sleep at all yesternight—the pity of it!" Rajee made infinite fun taking the usual liberty that was hers.

"Those who came to scoff remained to pray," Rangan preferred a classic quotation to his own energetic words.

Kandan, wishing to end the light banter on the eve of the most fateful day, said very quietly, "I'll state the dream and leave you to draw your own inferences. It's, I think, capable of several interpretations, and none sure."

"As all dreams are—and that is their virtue," Rangan made the preliminary interpretation with an astute face.

Kandan began in a serious voice. Everyone drew near him with vivid interest. "It was just five minutes to four, very early dawn. I dreamt intensely, the body perspired heavily and the heart-beats almost stopped, and the pulse sank the coldest. A giant figure towering the sky, neither very fierce nor very lovely, but just like a dark and beautiful cloud in the broad shape of a man with head and body, hands and eyes, stood from earth to heaven and seemed to bridge the sky with one stride. He was smiling, and had a long, long whip in hand. He came slowly, advancing from yonder little island in the river—millions of his myrmidons, dwarfs from the underworld held before him torchlights to light his way from heaven and show his celestial pomp."

"Was he riding?" Sarasvati eagerly asked.

"Yes, he was riding on a ridiculously small—"

"Buffalo?" Sarasvati completed the picture in a trembling voice.

"No, Sarasvati, no, not a buffalo, but a ridiculously small hippopotamus—herds of them I've seen quite as a boy now many years ago in Africa. The giant riding his ridiculous horse, carelessly descended from the sky and emerged more fully and rode straight to the railway station. He stroked his long, long lash from up in the sky, and the end of the whip just touched the funnel of the smoking engine—No. 4 was waiting, ready to start to Mayavaram—and the engine capsized like a toy—I felt I was the station-master of Tranquebar and I wailed to the giant on bended knees that I would lose my job for this. He took pity upon me, the pigmy, and with another easy stroke of the lash restored the capsized engine to the rails. Then he serenely rode further north and reached the river on the other side of the railway track and paused a moment surveying the scene as if to fix his route. He stroked his lash once again idly in the air—then there came such a sudden burst of choice fragrance as if the whole sea were converted into a lake of the finest *attar* of roses. I cried in wonder and joy."

Kandan wiped off the profuse flow of perspiration which even the mere recital of the dream caused, and continued in a steadier voice.

"Then he waded along the river—it was knee-deep to his little animal, and the hippopotamus swam like fish. The giant's head was in the cloud up in the sky, but you could see him smiling tenderly all the way, occasionally muttering a word of direction or two. Then he reached the mouth of the river and seemed to rest for a while on this very huge log of wood I have floated down just now—and it seemed to sink under his weight deep into the sand. Then he suddenly plunged his horse with one leap into the depths of the sea, lashing to mountain heights the sleeping waves of early dawn—then he stood towering high a furlong off in the sea just in front of the fort, and threw a scorching look of scorn at sleeping me, raised the whip and cracked it—it cut me to the quick somewhere here very near my heart—I suddenly woke up, and saw it was all only a terrific dream, a frightful apparition—never, never in my life have I had such a dream. Immediately I left my bed—you were all quite asleep—I ran out into the open, and the full moon was shining bright, pouring steadily comfort into my broken heart."

"I apprehend some dire calamity, Kanda. Ranga, cancel the meeting," Sarasvati said breaking the icy silence.

"No, no, never, Sarasvati, for an excited dream of mine—no such foolish step that would demoralise us, and impair for all time our gift for work. Rangan seems to be correct in his guess that the Collector of Tanjore would take no notice of this meeting at Tranquebar, almost a deserted island! I think the meeting will pass off very quietly—after all, it's a very small affair in the life of a nation. But we must immediately set to work on some plan, draw a programme of work—"

"A five-year plan or a ten-year plan?" Rajee finished the speech.

"Yes, I know Rajee's plans and ideas; they are quite in tune with mine. What are yours, Ranga—the work for the morrow after the meeting."

"Yes, Kandan is always wise and foresighted and his patriotic mind runs into true constructive ways. Let us prepare the plan of work for the future. To make a New India that will last for ever, a blessing to the poor and hungry millions—a five-year plan of hard and honest work on progressive lines. Let us sit now round yonder sand-dune." Rangan spoke with a new sense of dignity and faith in work.

On the top of the sand-dune grew a cluster of sea-weeds. Their sharp shoots waved in the air like a new, green flag flapping in the wind.

(4)

'Ah! Ranga, what is Swaraj worth," Kandan exclaimed as soon as the little group had settled down to a listening mood, "if it does not mean freedom to everyone of the three hundred and fifty millions, even the humblest, to grow to his fullest in his own land? We should work for a Swaraj that would bring out from each his best, in all the patterns of God's own infinite variety, both in the inner and the outer life of the individual, and reward each with the fruits of Nature according to his needs, the needs of a simple and pure life. Then only this sacred land of *Bharatavarsha* will be sacred in deed, as it is now in legend."

"Yes, Kanda, the greatest danger is that the vineyard of liberty reclaimed, tilled, and pruned by the labour of the patriot, and manured with the blood of the unknown volunteer may be annexed at harvest time by a few at the top, the merchant, the landlord, and the usurer. They may use the gathered power against their own fellowmen and exploit the million poor. That must be made impossible in our Swaraj." Rangan spoke with the untutored strength of native feeling.

"Yes, Ranga," Rajee said, almost moved to tears, "as you have so often spoken eloquently in London —the Indian problem is the problem of the poor who have been kept poor all through the ages. Its vast man-power given by God as a sacred gift to earth is wasted most pitifully like autumn leaves on the roadside suffering a perpetual dust-storm. Swaraj must give this vast man-power both scope and direction and save it from being wasted or exploited."

"And not till then will India know true peace," Rangan chimed in and surveyed with glowing eyes the tranquil charm of nature around him. "The evil that paralyses our life, Kanda, is not our religious or tribal discords but the most iniquitous and irresponsible system of land-tenure which sucks the blood of the poor in a hundred ways, and all toil goes to feed only the parasite. The hand that works in the mud and mire of the field only labours as an eternal coolie hand, and gathers the golden grains of the harvest only for a callous overlord's bank account and spendthrift life. The shrivelled hand that plucks the cotton on miles and miles of rich, black acres

-does not own even a piece of cloth to cover the shame of a slave's birth, not even a rag to wipe the tears of sorrow that come welling up the eyes at the sight of famished children at home. Sweated labour for another, Kanda, is the most ancient sorrow of man, but in this sacred land it is the most bitter salt-sea flood, as we have lost our freedom both within and without."

"Ranga, your indictment is true. No doubt, we occasionally produce giants like our own Himalayan peaks," Rajee spoke in a similar vein caught in Rangan's stream of fancy, "but our average level is but the low level of malarial swamps where no healthy life can be lived."

"We lack energy, the active kindliness and the co-operative will and the public virtues that make civic life a pleasure and an aid to individual fulfilment." Rangan emphasised his points with appropriate gestures delighted that his mind was at last gripping details of central significance instead of vague idealism with which he was so often charged. "There is a yawning gulf of apathy between the young and the old in this unhappy land, and we lack the thread of a common interest that knits the loose and scattered flowers into a garland of worship for the Mother. The elder does not take in hand the younger in an atmosphere of trust and freedom. The elder does not give his experience to guide and enrich the younger, and the younger does not give his loyalty in return. And we have remained slaves for lack of this single civic virtue, and every generation lives and dies like frogs in a cesspool of their own."

Rangan finished fervidly, and turning to Kandan said, "Yes, Kanda, you are right; I'm converted to your view. The glory of words is nothing before the glory of deeds. We must work selflessly if we want to win our own self-respect; we must make the most solid use of the energy these renascent times have set free."

"Yes, Ranga, we must build our Swaraj in such a way," Kandan warmly approved, "that we produce no brokers at the top, like worms in cheese, who deal carelessly with the lives of millions. The tyrant and the coward shall not grow in this ancient land of courage and love. The difficulty is not in getting Swaraj; for we are surely getting it. For ours is now a fight to the finish; to live or die as a nation. The test of our new life is not only in winning freedom but in applying it selflessly and courageously to the freedom of all, even the humblest in the land."

"Then, do you think, Kanda, that Swaraj will be easily got?"

"Easily got in the sense that it would be surely got, sooner or later. For, mark me, when a whole nation is struggling with one mind for freedom none can keep it back for long, not even the gods. A nation's freedom is like the swell of the sea—once it rises, no bunds on the shore, no land-marks, or sand-dunes of repression, can limit its flow, but everything will be flooded till—"

"Do you think that this wave of unrest now, Kanda, will soon become the swell of the sea?"

"Why this doubting question, Ranga? Watch intently the tremor on the crest of the waves that reach the shore and the deep moan of the mid-sea. This swell is Swaraj."

"If the wind but favours!"

"Why, surely, it will; only our pilots must be ready with the sails, and the captain watchful, keen-sighted and patient at the rudder to steer clear of many sunken rocks and shoals. For, Ranga, our Indian problem is unique in many ways both in bulk and in quality. It is a sub-continent which we are now trying to fuse into a political unity—imagine the several States of Europe uniting under one Government! India has achieved a unity higher than the political, the unity of the spirit that arises out of a common culture and philosophy. But now this higher urge in man is sought to be yoked to the utilitarian wheel of politics, so that what collects now as so many little communal pools of virtue at different levels on the rugged slopes of life may meet each other and flow together into a broad and common river, each sharing in the life and joy of another. But to make this dream of a renascent India possible, politics itself should suffer a sea-change."

"What do you mean by sea-change, Kanda, it is a poetic word and may mean anything."

"In its simplest sense, a change for the higher, a change in quality. Politics are wooden now. The motives of action should be spiritualised. The old system that goes to make the rich richer and the poor poorer must be broken up from its very foundations, and the nation's energy moved along new channels, feeding all the plants and trees alike, so that each may share in and get according to its needs the full benefits of Nature, and put forth its own finest flowers—"

"Kanda, you too have begun to talk like Rangan. Is it the result of the dream or of Rangan's influence? Everything sounds so nice and uplifting as words,—but how are you going to translate them into action and apply them to the chaos and struggle of the day?" Rajee asked, striking a vigorous note of realism into the airy flight of winged words.

"If I understand Kandan aright," Rangan began to explain, "to illustrate his ideas with a figure, politics is but the generating centre that transmits the energy to the hundred wheels that roll, big and small, each grinding its own share of work, uniting at the end to weave the fine fabric of social life."

"Rangan's words add only confusion to the chaos," Rajee said in her own irrepressible way.

But Kandan came to the rescue and approved the commentary. "Rangan is right, Rajee, that's just what I meant. Politics are a mere distributing media of power, and by themselves quite lifeless like the leather-strap in a factory. But in actual life the administrators, the distributing media of the power, are not dead matter but active, living men with a little initiative and purpose of their own, by which they pervert the power meant for the common good to their own selfish ends, and fail to pass the life current to where it is most needed."

"Well, then, why don't you sketch a perfect scheme to be worked out immediately after Rangan's meeting this evening?" Rajee asked sincerely.

"It's the easiest thing in the world to sketch an ideal polity—it has been the work and play of many since the days of Plato. But to work up the ideals into an active social order you want a body of workers, pure and devoted, till the ideals expressed in action become part of our being. We want a *sanyasin* order to whom compassion, the joy of service and selflessness come as native as drops of honey to the flower. Men like Gandhiji, instead of being a world-phenomenon to be worshipped like the sun, must grow on every hedge like blackberries. At least every village must have one Gandhiji working for its renovation till it is restored to healthy life and needs no Gandhiji for a trumpet call to pure, selfless public work."

"Like Kandan," Sarasvati applauded.

"Yes, like Kandan. But you talk of Swaraj, Kanda, as if Swaraj has been gained and it is now in the hollow of your hand?" Rajee asked.

"Where is Swaraj, Rajee; it does not lie outside you. It lies in you, it lies with you; it lies within you!"

"It's nice and charming as a merely verbal philosophy. But Great Britain won't yield to all these hypnotic *mantras.*"

"They will yield, Rajee, the moment they know from the ring of your own peaceful words that you mean what you say. The sun-dried men here may think that aeroplanes and machine-guns can keep in the pen for all time the hungry millions. But the world is not really ruled by them. Our answer to them is: the only power on earth that can conquer and lay at rest violence is non-violence, even as water alone can quench fire. Peace alone can finally win war. War never really does but always prepares for another, wider and bigger war. It drives hate deeper into the heart, even as violence drives but deeper a random thorn in the flesh."

Kandan paused a moment and spoke again in measured words: "From what I read of the signs in the sky, Swaraj is certain. No power on earth can deny it to us but ourselves. The seeming discords of the day, of tribe and religion, will close into kinship like the dark scattered clouds that close their serried ranks in the monsoon hour when the wild winds play the horn of thunder, and sound the march of descending rains."

Kandan cleared his voice and continued, "Great Britain herself needs to be friends with India. She has forty millions to feed, and her patriotic soil can feed but fifteen. How long can she go on feeding the other twenty-five millions by selling cotton goods, coal and hardware to a world that has already learnt to produce its own primary agricultural needs, each country within its own frontiers—her problem can be solved only by a large scheme of emigration—but her statesmen are now burying their heads in the dry sands of party politics and petty triumphs, and see not the true path to light and freedom. The days of narrow nationalism are over. The future Government of man shall be carried on only by two agencies—the League of Nations and the village *panchayat* or the urban Council. Decentralisation shall be complete and life-giving."

"Then you mean, Kanda, the attitude to life should fundamentally change, if all that you say should come to pass. Everyone should feel that his neighbour is as sacred as himself and love him as he loves himself," thoughtfully Rangan added his commentary. "All the religions have preached it these two thousand years and more, and Christianity the most, but practised it the least. That is why the result is so barren and conflicting, and the weeds have overrun the garden, and the West is deeply entangled in a vicious circle of hate and strife."

Sarasvati who watched in silence the discourse, said: "The best service to our land will be to show the real way by setting up one village, and working it out perfectly on the true model. From what I see we have here a pure *sanyasin* order for public work—let us consecrate five years to that work before we think of anything else. Give me, Kanda, in your utmost hour of thought, a five-year plan to work a village into a perfect idyll of life. If one such blossoms into life, I'll know then, from a solitary flower, that this stagnant pool of Indian life is truly a lotus-pond and not an *alli* ditch. I'll then patiently wait for many more lotus-buds to bloom in due time. Pray, Kanda, give us a plan of work—the meeting of this evening will come and go fading in an hour like the red, red *anthimallika* flower that blossoms at five and dies at six in the evening."

Sarasvati's voice had a glorious cadence but it was charged with a strange melancholy.

"Kanda, accept me," Padma spoke with the spirit of real dedication, "as one of your group for work. Though young, I'll labour hard my best."

"Padma, why this request?" Sarasvati replied to Padma, "you are already one of us. Without young men like you, how can the country hope to do real work in any field."

"Pray, Kanda, begin with my village." Chockalinga laid his all at the feet of Kandan and Sarasvati. "It now belongs to you and the whole world by virtue of a higher title."

"Then, Chockalinga, may God bless you! Yours is a sacrifice all too rare in the annals of modern India. Yes, let us prepare a plan, and work and live only for it till the freedom of our land is won. In the cocoanut garden where the very toddy-shop stood, Ranga, let us consecrate an *ashrama*, an order of men devoted to the Indian Rural Service. All the aids of science, the thoughts of philosophy, the blessings of religion, the beauty of arts and literature that make men like gods, I would bring to the threshold of every cottage in script that it can understand and in deeds that it can enjoy. Under true Swaraj, every Indian village will be free, autonomous and perfect like an atom that holds in its tiny bosom the whole range of cosmic power."

"Can we not work up a village, Kanda, thoroughly ignoring the existing political conditions?" Rajee asked with a real desire.

"Quite possible, Rajee, that's just what we'll try;—only we require a noble and fearless order of men and a very high average among the common folk—pure, selfless, self-controlled like the links of a chain, every link even and equally strong. Then we can ignore the environment; then fetters lose their hold, and we march on to both individual and collective self-realisation;—these excrescent growths will fall off, lacking the impurities to feed upon. For such ideal work you must produce a social order which won't give birth to a single broker who would sell for a mess of pottage his precious, undivided share in the comman heritage."

"That is really a state of perfection you are preaching, Kanda, in which there would be no need for one man to rule or work for another—all government would become unnecessary—"

"Quite so, Rajee, but that is the spiritual aim of all government; govern so well that you need so little of it. The reason for all action is that man may ultimately be liberated from action. Is it not? Even as the final aim of life is that you may be released from life for all time. That's the spiritual urge in man. Without this harmonising view, all our activities, social, political or economic, will be but diffuse, unrelated, disruptive, wasteful, injurious, and all pursuits illusory. There will be no joy in deeds or words, no rhythm in life, no effort to understand the nature of reality."

"Quite so, Kanda," Sarasvati said, and Rangan and Rajeswari nodded assent. Kandan paused a moment, driving his fingers into the sand.

"Rajee, there is only one approach to all pure, good and noble work, as you yourself told me one evening before this very sea. *Brahmacharya* alone can lead us on to victory in the cause to which we are wedded. Touch no great work till you are fit in mind for this self-conquest and purity. This control of the senses and the slow rendering of the carnal energy in man into the divine power, will bring us *Atmagnanam*, a cosmic consciousness compared with which the gift of reason and intelligence would seem but a toy-gift to a child. Till Swaraj is won, let us take this vow, Ranga and Rajee—and Sarasvati is far above us, she needs no urge to acquire a virtue that has come to her as a cradle gift,—Padma, Kamakshi and Chockalinga, something tells me of a common run of life for you. Join us and work with us till Swaraj is won. God will bless us. Let us do our duty for the day as the time-spirit moves us, and the fruits will take care of themselves."

There was tense silence for a moment and the group sat deeply immersed in thought.

The morning sun had slowly mounted up. The sea had already begun to ebb and the current was now flowing down the river. The stately log of wood had also floated down, and was being buffeted about by the eddies and cross-currents at the very narrow mouth of the river where the water churned and foamed, circling round and round.

Ponnan came rushing along the sea-shore, and even at a distance it could be seen that something serious was the matter that moved him to this unusual racing flight on heavy sand.

(5)

" Master, master, a battalion of three hundred Malabar police reserves have arrived with fixed bayonets and rifles. Our things have been unceremoniously thrown out of the fort, and they are now bleaching in the sun. I also hear that they are going to prohibit the meeting."

" Any more news, Ponna ? " Kandan asked, and Rangan felt as he once felt at the Egmore third-class booking-office window.

"But already a thousand people from all parts of the District have come—and our Mudaliar's men have come in fine array, five hundred strong, all clothed in khaddar and marching under the leadership of Nallan and Nochi."

"I feared trouble all along, nothing like quiet work, Ranga," Sarasvati spoke in a subdued tone.

"I'll manage the whole thing; I'm not afraid of police turbans." Rangan though uneasy at heart spoke with assurance. "Leave it to me, Sarasu, I'll manage the whole affair very quietly. Evidently the police badly needed a change to the sea-side. They are glad of the chance I have given them."

Mr. Mudaliar was indignant, but Kandan cautioned him to be calm. The small group broke up immediately, hearts heavy.

Kandan looked around as if in search of something. He gazed intently at the sea that glittered in the blazing shine of the morning sun. He was surprised but delighted to find the heavy log of wood floating along with him very near the shore, proudly ascending and descending wave after wave, as if it had also decided to attend Rangan's public meeting and give its vote in his favour.

CHAPTER XIX

THE HOUR OF FATE

(1)

A SENTINEL, with a drawn bayonet, was posted at each of the gates of the fort which looked lively after so many years of desolation. It seemed to have gained at last her bridal day of martial activity.

The District Superintendent of Police, dead tired after sixty miles of continuous drive in a Ford car on the dusty, bumping road from Tanjore to Tranquebar, flung himself into an easy chair in the central hall of the fort. The Deputies, the Inspectors, and the Subs of four Taluks lined round him with bated breath and whispering humbleness.

Khan Bahadur Meera Sahib was there with his flowing beard and refined hawk-like features. He was the direct descendant of a soldier of fortune from Central Asia who distinguished himself in the famous siege of Ginjee in the time of Aurangazebe, for which he was rewarded with a *jagir*.

Rao Bahadur Vedagiri Iyer was also there with his faultless Brahmin features and twinkle of intelligence, somewhat sun-burnt and roughened by police discipline and hard work, ever ready and alert to prove at a moment's notice his loyalty to the salt he had eaten.

Rao Sahib Ratnam Pillai too was there, a young man but a darling of fortune with fine rolling eyes, and a beautifully trained moustache that grew luxuriantly like *nanal* grass on the fertile banks of the Cauvery, which keeps the fretting waters from chafing the banks. The Rao Sahib was a happy by-product of dyarchy. He entered the police ranks as an ordinary head-constable. But in the tumble of elections under the new dispensation, his own brother-in-law became Minister for Development. Under his fostering care, Rao Sahib Ratnam Pillai, like the mango tree in the street magic, developed quickly from a constable into a Deputy Superintendent of Police with a title on the New Year's day.

Khan Bahadur Meera Sahib, of course, depended more on his ancestry, the long-lasting and never-to-be forgotten valour which his adventurous ancestor had displayed at the siege of Ginjee. He had also the good fortune of being born a Muhammadan in South India, and his rise was as sure as that of the morning sun to meridian heights. It was also rumoured that he, the Khan Bahadur, would become the D. S. P. at the next vacancy.

As for Vedagiri, he was found to be one of the indispensible Brahmins in any scheme of life. He had done such excellent work for his masters that nobody could really ignore and keep him down in the lower rungs of the police ladder for any great length of time.

(2)

"What do you think of the situation, Khan Bahadur? I fear the Mudaliar has commandeered the whole Taluq into Tranquebar. Very foolish of him to have joined this movement! Why this huge crowd? Does Rangaswami know Tamil? I'm told he is going to address in English in which he is an expert. How many here in this crowd, you think, know English—barely a dozen I should think." The D. S. P. rolled his tongue very complacently. He had just finished a very hearty breakfast and Tranquebar was justly famous for its fine fish. He was feeling and talking so pleasantly that nobody could have said that he had come out on a critical errand but for the thickening and excited crowd in the *maidan*.

"It's all mere show, sir—nothing will come out of it. I rather think we should have quietly ignored this meeting; especially you, sir, need not have come all the way from Tanjore for this. I could manage it—why, our head-constable Tandavarayan says he would manage the whole affair with half-a-dozen men." The Khan Bahadur decorously managed his broken English, and the D. S. P. was rather impresssed by his commonsense point of view.

"I respectfully beg to differ from my friend, the Khan Bahadur," Rao Bahadur Vedagiri began to ingratiate himself against his rival for the headship of the District. "I come from this very Taluk, sir—I know these wild men who gave no end of trouble to the Danish Government. Mr. Mudaliar, though burly, is at heart, when provoked, a very courageous man; and he is a very great influence with these wild men, and his word is law to them. It was but last week they looted twenty-thousand *kalams* of paddy all in one hour, looted their own *pannai*. Sir, you have done the most proper and foresighted thing in having made these adequate arrangements and brought the Malabar reserves."

"I rather agree with you on the whole, Vedagiri. Rao Bahadur is an old fox, you know, Khan Bahadur." The D. S. P. complimented the Rao Bahadur, and pleasantly laughed, belching profusely.

Rao Sahib Ratnam Pillai, of course, could not display any special powers on this critical occasion; neither his local knowledge—for he was a Tinnevelly man—nor his tongue. But everything has its own compensation in Nature. He rolled his eyes in flashes of special police anger, and stroked the moustache and trimmed it at both the ends into fine lance-heads as a gesture of courage and deeds that were his lot in life. He rolled his eyes as if he would burn the whole of Tranquebar with his look of fire.

"Still, Khan Bahadur," the D. S. P. gave his final orders, "now that we have made the fullest arrangements, see that the situation is well in hand and nothing untoward happens. As Vedagiri says these are wild men, and I myself know Mr. Mudaliar well enough—poor chap why and how has he drifted into this muddle, I wonder? You know the meeting has been prohibited under Section 144. The Divisional Magistrate of Mayavaram will be here in half-an-hour. You made a mistake in the morning. As soon as you came here you should have cleared this *maidan* of all men, women, and children—now it would be difficult—several hundreds have crowded now—"

"I suggested so in the morning to my friend, the Khan Bahadur," Vedagiri softly exclaimed and tried to insinuate himself.

The Khan Bahadur simply looked at him in wonder, sniffing contemptuously.

"Well, let that go, now post a few alert fellows at the entrance to the town itself, and block more men coming in, adding to the excitement and the confusion; I'm dead tired, Khan Bahadur; I'll take a little rest now. The meeting at five? I hope it won't take place and Rangan won't disobey the order —and force us to needless action."

"Yes, sir, we will attend to the minutest detail—you may take rest, sir, after the long and tedious drive," said Rao Bahadur Vedagiri, in a fine coaxing voice—for he too was in the same grade as the Khan Bahadur and expected to act as the D. S. P. when the chance came.

The Khan Bahadur also followed the good example of the D. S. P. and retired for a nap. For he had also had a really hearty breakfast. Nothing like a little nap after that!

Poor Vedagiri felt that the whole burden fell on him though he was not the Deputy of the place, but the Khan Bahadur. But he cheerfully accepted it as it gave him a chance to show his superior organising power and police insight. He reckoned all possible and impossible emergencies and tried to provide against them.

His very manœuvres kindled the ire of the idle crowd waiting for the speech and the meeting. They were becoming more and more fretful and excited.

Nandan, Mookkan, and Katteri, Irullan, Karuppan, and Irullappan, were itching at the hand for a counter-stroke, and looked with love at the debris of an old house and the heaps of broken bricks that lay around in inviting confusion, idle and ready for many years.

(3)

It was a little vineyard in front of a beautiful old bangalow. The vines were as old as seventy summers and they bore luscious bunches of grapes. Ponnan and Kamakshi sat under their inviting shade and fell into an eager conversation with each other. Ponnan was all tremulous excitement.

"Ponna, why all this tremendous array of police force for such a simple rustic meeting as ours? Three hundred policemen with gleaming bayonets and loaded guns! You know why all this—you are a townsman and must know these things. Mere threat? or something dire will happen to us all? What harm is there in Rangan speaking and telling us the current news?" Kamakshi very innocently and playfully asked Ponnan.

But Ponnan was in a very disturbed state of mind. He was moving about hither and thither the whole day, and was wearied.

"Kamakshi, quick of insight so native to your sex, your fears are well-founded. I too apprehend some trouble. Mudaliar's men are all excitable and if his person be but roughly handled, as is but likely in a huge crowd with three hundred policemen to regulate its peace, his Nandans, Mookkans and Katteris will all come out with brick-bats—Tranquebar with all its dilapidated houses is full of these missiles, so temptingly full—and then the result you don't know, Kamakshi, the police will open fire—brick-bats will be answered by bullets, and blood will flow like water—"

Kamskshi shuddered at the thought. She felt very near fainting.

"Ponna, you fear some calamity to our friends and masters?"

"Yes, I fear, Kamakshi; nay, I'm almost sure. The turn the events have taken this morning is unexpected, and all the materials for an explosion are gathering quickly,—in half-an-hour we can't even escape from here, Kamakshi. The way in and out, is already barricaded. And more on your account, Kamakshi, I'm terribly afraid," Ponnan closed in a low, husky voice, tenderly looking at her.

"Why on my account, Ponna?" Kamakshi hesitatingly asked. For she, the shrewd girl, read to some extent the language of his eyes. Ponnan was still young and bore handsome and refined features.

"Is't not clear to you yet, my pretty bird—I love you, deeply and tenderly love you. I adore you. There is no joy for me on earth till I marry you and call you my own for ever. From the very first day I set eyes on you at Akkur, I've never taken them off. My heart is throbbing, Kamakshi—"

"Very strange, Ponna, that you should feel for me like this. I'm lonely, poor—"

"So all the more I seek you and love you—"

"Ponna, I don't as yet feel the call of love or marriage—a rustic girl like me, what do I know of these—my *maman* is my master in this matter. Ponna, don't ask of me to do the impossible."

"Kamakshi, will you give the same indifferent answer if instead of me Padma now proposes to you and confesses his love."

Kamakshi deeply blushed as she had never blushed before. Ponnan saw it and realised at once the truth of his bold charge. He added with a violent clench of his fist, biting his lips, "That shall never happen, Kamakshi. It's a crime against the very foundations of our Hindu society. You and Padma are born far too apart to come and mingle together."

. Ponnan with superb art watched the effect of his well-planned words. Kamakshi was deeply perturbed and felt like an eagle shot by an arrow in its highest eagle-flights—an arrow into the heart.

"Do but pass your word, Kamakshi." Ponnan implored again, "I love you intensely—in half-an-hour this *maidan* will become the scene of bloodshed and riot—there's only one way of escaping out of this—tell me, Kamakshi, I'll brave it out for your sake ; we shall escape. There lies a catamaran there, ready and fit, hidden amid those ruins from the eyes of these men—we will take to it even now and sail away to safety from this danger zone—to Tirumalaivasal, but ten miles off, to live for ever there under the eternal shade of the cocoanut, listening to the lisp of the sea. Kamakshi, I'll follow you wherever you ask me to. Kamakshi, I'm at your feet." Ponnan implored passionately.

Kamakshi stood terrified, unable to speak, heavily perspiring.

(4)

Fortunately Chockalinga himself came into the seclusion of the vineyard at the right moment searching for Kamakshi. Kamakshi was relieved of her embarrassment.

"Poona, Kamakshi and you plotting together! Why are you hiding in this safe corner under the vines? I thought you were a town-rat, not afraid of police red-turbans."

"No, no, not at all,—only I was saying to Kamakshi I feared that something untoward may happen to-day—so many police tigers, penned in a fort with bayonets and *lathis*, may not remain idle. Mr. Mudaliar, one request I make most humbly—kindly ask Nallan and Nochi to keep our men under control. Some random or playful act may provoke the police—"

"May provoke what? You mean to say I'm afraid of these red turbans? The D. S. P. is my friend and has tasted my princely hospitality many a time. He may not be now openly with me—even if he be against me, I'm no coward like you, Ponna. I'm not afraid of these red turbans and khaki shorts—my men, at one stroke of my eyelids, will sweep them out into the sea, clean—"

"Master, pray don't do any such rash act. The police are armed to the teeth. The D. S. P. and the Khan Bahadur are very hard and business-like men if it comes to that, and Vedagiri has his eye only on promotion—they may all be your friends in fair weather as guests, but not in trouble. Master, pray listen to Ponnan's humble but wise and cautious words and keep to this corner,—Ponnan though young knows the world, especially the police world."

"Ponna, it's very unmanly advice that you are giving me when our friends are in the very thick of the fight."

But Ponnan implored Chockalinga in entreaty. And before Kamakshi he seemed to kneel in worship. In this beautiful hour of prayer Chockalinga detected a wonderful similarity in the faces of Kamakshi and Ponnan, a common outline as if the two flowers were of the same stem and came of a common seed.

Chockalinga had been noticing this curious resemblance for some time and in this juxtaposition it was very clear, the resemblance. Chockalinga asked with a smile: "You both look like brother and sister in this hour of peril. Ponna, you say you are a distant cousin of Kandan—you come from this Taluq, and you remember your village?"

"Memadur."

"Memadur?" cried in the same voice Kamakshi and Chockalinga.

"Ponna, your father's name?" Chockalinga asked again.

"*Peria Pannai* Vythilinga Mudaliar!"

"*Peria Pannai* Vythilinga Mudaliar!"

Two voices blended into one in glad but incredulous surprise.

"Then, I'm your sister" Kamakshi cried overpowered by emotion.

"Yes, Kamakshi, then you are the sister of Ponnan," Chockalinga spoke with real comfort at the success of his own happy surmise. "I've known you, Kamakshi, as a little girl at your *maman's* house—and your father too was a friend of ours—he was struck with inconsolable grief at the loss of his runaway boy, his only boy; and the common impression here is that Ponnan was kidnapped even as a little boy of seven by a wandering troupe of bear-trainers. Your mother and father died broken-hearted leaving you homeless as a pretty little child at the mercy of your *maman*—you remember, Ponna, anything of your early days now?"

"Mr. Mudaliar, I remember a few terrible things as if in a dream, but the romance of my life must make a story of its own—it can't be told in an hour or a day, and not now in this excited hour. I'm glad at last I've met my sister, on this fateful day, the one relation of mine on earth; and she is Kamakshi."

Ponnan could not finish his speech; he was overpowered, and he gazed in speechless wonder at Kamakshi's bird-like beauty. It assumed for him a new significance and joy.

Kamakshi nestled near Ponnan, joy haloing her face.

(5)

"What's the uproar there? Go out and see, Ponna. The tumult seems to increase—"

Ponnan went out quickly. For now he was even more anxious for their safety.

Chockalinga availed himself of the inviting solitude and the lonely charms of Kamakshi and flung his arms in a posture of loving entreaty before her and began: "Ever since I saw you, Kamakshi, my heart has never been at rest. Assure me now of your love from your own lips—I'll cheerfully wait for years to deserve it—do penance on rocks and hills, dales and rivers—nay, court imprisonment for the country's cause. Pray, don't say 'no,' Kamakshi—to win you, I'll even risk my life for the freedom of the country if that pleases you."

Kamakshi stood utterly bewildered, motionless like a bird which has wheeled to its highest flights in the sky and knows not its place or mind.

But outside the walled-in garden the uproar was increasing. Ponnan returned running in breathless haste with a strange look of terror in his face. "Pray, Mr. Mudaliar—it's impossible to be safe here—my words are coming true; events are shaping themselves as I feared. Quite too late to save my master Rangan, and Rajeswari, or Kandan and Sarasvati—they are in the thick of the crowd—the whole mass is seething with excitement, and the slighest friction will bring out the explosion—I've seen many such crowds in my varied life—this is most terrible in its rustic splendour and force. Though the main entrances are closed with policemen, the crowd is thickening quick on the *maidan*, for the men, women, and children are pouring into through many devious ways and by-lanes,—who can stop a crowd intent on coming into an open town like Tranqueber."

"Ponna, come to the point, what is the matter?"

"Evidently Rangan will speak—and they are all going to disobey the order—the result will be disaster—the police will open fire and there will be severe *lathi* and bayonet charges—for this is not an urban crowd, and your wild fellows will be afraid of neither steel nor fire. There are ten thousand people in the *maidan* packed like *kola* fish; and another ten thousand outside the walls of the city-gate, shut out by a strong police force guarding the entrance. This beautiful open will become shambles in half-an-hour, and blood will flow like a river to the sea, alas, for nothing!"

"Well, then, what is it that you say, Ponna? suggest a way out of the difficulty."

"Let us escape to the sea; that is the only way out—yonder amid the temple ruins on the sea-shore, a catamaran is waiting for us. Let us escape to the sea before it is too late. In an hour, we can clear ten miles by the coast and the wind is with us—Mr. Mudaliar, pray follow me, and you, Kamakshi."

Padma rushed in in great haste. He came in time to hear the closing speech of Ponnan and cried, casting a tender look of love on Kamakshi, "Fie, fie upon you, Ponna, wasting your time idly under the shade of vines and scheming to sneak out while your friends are courageously fighting the country's cause. We have resolved to disobey the order. Rangan and Rajee, and all of us are searching for you, sir, Mr. Mudaliar. Make haste. Your presence will restore order in the crowd. They are all excited —especially your *pannai* fellows."

"Fie, fie, Ponna, I agree with Padma and his courageous words. Your plan of escape at a critical time as this brings dishonour to your father Vythilinga's name—he was the bravest man in the Taluq by common consent." Chockalinga spoke with the ease and dignity of a born nobleman. "Running away, deserting your master and friends just at the hour when they need you most! Ponna, Kandan too is a remote agnate of mine—though we have lost touch with each other for generations—Well, at this critical hour I should not stand on ceremony. I shall go and see the D.S.P. We are very good friends, though the country's cause divides us now. Let me think of an honourable way out of this madding crowd—this has far exceeded my expectations; that only shows that there is so much of patriotic feeling in the country. Yes, I must move out immediately, Kamakshi, and pacify this excited throng. Ponna, look to the safety of your sister and try to reach Rangan and Kandan safely—or be here, that's better. Don't tarry behind, Padma, come with me. I need your presence."

"Take care of your steps, Mr. Mudaliar, and in the excitement of the crowd pray don't do any hasty deed." Ponnan begged as he really wanted to shape a way out of the impending peril.

When Chockalinga passed out of sight, Kamakshi cried, "Ponna, I can take care of myself in this safe corner. Follow Mr. Mudaliar and Padma and guide them through. None can protect them better in this hour of peril than you, my brother."

Chockalinga for all his aristocratic ease and laziness was young and brave, and Tranquebar was the soil of his forefathers for over eleven generations, and they were the uncrowned kings of this sea-resort under the Danish rule. Chockalinga felt his pride wounded that evening in the unnecessary display of police force. He remembered that his ancestors too were once military chieftains, charged with the guardianship of the marches of the Coleroon. His young blood boiled with pride and indignation.

Chockalinga in this defiant frame of mind, swaggered into the crowd which instinctively opened out a winding passage to him, the premier nobleman of the Taluq. Chockalinga wanted only to see his friend, the D.S.P., who would have been the first to see him under normal circumstances, just to tell the police chief that he would stand guarantee for the peace of the place, and all this police array and fright was wholly unnecessary and that even if Rangan disobeyed the order the British Raj would not come tumbling down and that he, the D.S.P. of a district, could well afford to watch with amusement the verbal fire-works of the evening.

(6)

Hardly had Padma and Chockalinga emerged from the seclusion of the vineyard when Padma met most unexpectedly his own brother, Raghu, in the very act of scrutinising the crowd as if in search for his brother.

Padma exclaimed in speechless wonder, " Raghu, Raghu ! " not believing his own eyes while Raghu almost fainted with joy at the sudden discovery of his lost brother.

Chockalinga stood a little way off, perplexed by his own thoughts.

" Move on, Mr. Mudaliar, I'll join you in a minute." Padma spoke hurriedly in excitement.

" Padma, don't tarry a minute longer than necessary with your friend," Chockalinga spoke with some agitation, at the same time slowly moving into the thickening crowd. " Though you are quite young, Padma, we all need you at this critical hour. Follow me wherever I may be the whole of this evening."

" Yes, Mr. Mudaliar, I'll be with you in a minute."

Chockalinga had literally to elbow out his way through the crowd. But he moved on not at all minding the unusual physical discomfort it meant to him. For he was intent on his own plan of action. He was astonished at the crowd that surged and thronged beyond expectation and asked himself, " Is the patriotic feeling so intense in the land ? "

Meanwhile Raghu and Padma fell into an eager conversation.

" Raghu, have you come all the way from Shiyali to attend this meeting ? Is mother feeling very much my flight ? How is Chandru doing ? Does he miss my kisses ? " Padma spoke in the soft voice of anxiety.

"Yes, indeed, Padma, mother is inconsolable,—and Chandru misses you very much. You might have at least sent us a card of safety."

"Yes, I might have, perhaps, but I have been so busy since I left you," Padma spoke with a faint smile and repeated his question, "Have you come here solely to attend the meeting or on some official business?"

"Official business? No. I've come, Padma, solely to attend your meeting in atonement for not attending yours the other day on the Uppanar river-bed. I heard a little while ago that Rangan and one Padma, a young boy, will be the top speakers of the evening. And I prayed to myself that it might be yourself, my own brother; I'm so proud of you, Padma?"

Padma could not understand this radical change in his brother but replied in utter sympathy, "Yes, yes, I too wanted to speak, brother, but the Collector has prohibited our meeting under Sec. 144. But we have decided to break the law and hold the meeting. The crowd is unexpectedly heavy and we apprehend trouble both from the police and the crowd—the whole thing is something like having fireworks in a godown where bales and bales of raw cotton are stocked—the result is certain conflagration. Let us move on, brother. Have you taken leave for a day or two?"

"I've taken leave, Padma, for all time. I've acted on your advice though a little late and resigned my menial job. I've from to-day joined a higher service, joined you and your friends to work for the freedom of the country."

"Impossible to believe you, brother. Yonder is our little group of leaders. See there, Kandan and Rangan, Rajeswari and Sarasvati. We'll join them now and do our best to keep the peace, and enforce some order in this madding crowd."

"Padma, order will come of its own accord when one of you begins to speak. Better the first speaker starts in Tamil---I think that from the nature of the crowd, not very many know English."

"Raghu, most probably I may be the first speaker if the police don't break us up before that —but how can they break up this huge crowd without slaughter and violence on a large scale?"

"Padma, look yonder this side towards the northern gate—there seems to be going on there some severe scuffle, if not a free fight between the crowd and the police."

"It seems so. Let us hurry up to the spot, brother."

Padma and Raghu, hand locked in hand, in warm fraternal clasp in the hour of peril and common service to the Mother, moved on quickly through the intricate maze of the crowd and joined the Rangan group which was also fast moving towards the storm centre.

The mere presence of Raghu gave Padma a giant's strength.

(7)

Meanwhile Chockalinga approached the entrance to the fort by the northern gate. There was a cordon of Malabar police—utter strangers to the land. They did not know him as the territorial magnate, the premier nobleman of the Taluq. They did not like his aristocratic swagger before the very bayonet-end of their rifles. Chockalinga announced curtly and pompously that he wanted to see the D.S.P., and moved on boldly without another word to enter the low gate. One constable, more cheeky than the rest, pushed him back with the ringed end of his *lathi* shouting at the same time in the sharp voice of command which never fell into Chockalinga's ears all these years of peace and plenty, "Keep out of the bayonet range, you burly fool, lest you tempt me to put an inch of cold steel into your rich flesh. Nobody can see the D.S.P. or enter the fort now—" He suitably adjusted his rifle-end for action to carry out the threat.

Nandan, Mookkan, and Katteri, Irullan, Karuppan, and Irullappan, Nochi, the stalwart *talayari*, and Govindan, Pavadai, and Nallan, grateful to the salt of ages they had eaten, and rich with the loot of twenty thousand *kalams* of paddy but last week, were standing at a respectful and loyal distance with their hordes of men. The moment they saw the undreamt of indignity to their master so roughly handled, they sprang like wounded tigers, and overpowered the sentry group of half-a-dozen. Meanwhile, Chockalinga was dragged, carried away to a place of safety by Nallan and Nochi.

The police whistle of alarm and distress flew from mouth to mouth disturbing the quiet nap of the D. S. P. and the Khan Bahadur. The enraged crowd began with brick-bats, that lay ready to hand in such profuse heaps all over seemingly waiting for the suppressed call of ages.

The ponderous Deputy Collector of Mayavaram in his loose shuffling trousers was there ready to quell the riot and put Rangan into jail. He warned the crowd of the apprehended breach of the peace and asked them to disperse in two minutes, or the police would have to use *lathi* charge and rifle-fire to break up the meeting and disperse the crowd. He screeched at the top of his voice as if he meant to the crows on the neighbouring banyan tree these words of warning, and asked once again the crowd gathered in thousands to disperse in two minutes.

How could ten thousand men who had collected there slowly from early dawn disperse in two minutes even at the risk of rifle-fire? And the way out was fully blocked—the raging sea to the east, the fort walls to the south, and a regular pile of buildings to the north and the west, with the main way out barricaded by the police. But the Deputy Collector thought only of his imminent duty in that distressed and panicky hour.

The *lathi* charge came: once, twice, thrice with all the harshness that could be at the end of a ringed stick, and failed. The police then opened fire: once, twice, thrice. Bullets flew in the air like white-ants flying in their bridal hour before death. Terrible cries went up to Heaven. Fortunately, the fort walls were uncomfortably high, and most of the bullets found their way in the air to the orchard that lay on the other side of the *maidan*. Bullets pierced grapes in bunches hanging in the vineyard, sweet pomegranate-buds, luscious graft mangoes just at their ripening time, and bananas in bending bunches.

Ponnan received a shot at the calf-muscle, but still moved on limping to where Kandan was standing, calm and collected. Still the bullets were flying about, everyone rushing hither and thither. But Rangan and Rajeswari, Kandan and Sarasvati stood their ground with wonderful calm and presence of mind.

Padma stood voluntarily covering Kandan. As if by magic he received in his own right palm a bullet that flew straight at Kandan's face. Padma cried and leaned on Raghu's shoulders in pain. Kandan moved on but a step to help Padma.

Suddenly a soft, mortal cry came tearing from the depths of flesh. Kandan staggered to the ground, lifting the right hand to the heart, pressing it hard there. A bullet had struck him very near his heart, just indeed where the lash of the giant in the dream cracked its stroking end. Kandan's kindly heart found room in his dying hour even for fatal lead, the lead that ends the life of a patriot but changes death into the deathless life of a martyr.

"Kanda, Kanda," ten thousand voices cried. The waves lashed in moaning fury. The log of wood in the sea tilted to the sky as if in humble prayer and for a last glimpse of the great patriot.

"My life is over, Rajee—it is a mortal shot—I knew my approaching end even this morning when the full moon poured comfort after the dream, and beckoned me to herself. I won't recover, Rajee. But my life will not be one lived in vain if only you all work together and carry out our plan, consecrating your life and love for the freedom of the country and the uplift of these down-trodden masses—foodless, homeless and hungry for ages."

Kandan paused a moment and continued with a slight flush of calm in his face, "Yes, Rajee, do marry Ranga; he is a noble soul, and his birth is a gain to our aching land. Chockalinga, on you rests everything, devote your life and wealth for the uplift of the poor—something tells me that Kamakshi will lead you to victory—marry that sweet, simple girl. Ponna, you too are purified. Chockalinga tells me Kamakshi is your sister; nothing can be happier."

After a moment's pause, Kandan turned to Padma, "you are my hope, Padma. Consecrate your life to the service and freedom of the Motherland. Think of nothing else but how to work out your love for the Motherland." And Kandan gently stroked Padma on his back, who kneeled in worship before him touching his feet.

"Ah! Sarasvati, I die peacefully," Kandan turned with great effort towards Sarasvati and said in a low voice, "I die happily; for I'm sure that the country's cause is sure and safe in your hands. None can break you or touch you, not even bullets. Guide our friends and teach them to live the higher life you live—and remember me in your prayers. Ah, ah——" Kandan bore bravely the pain of the coming end.

"Kanda, may we all have your blessings—if this tragic end be the will of God. We will think of no earthly pleasures till the freedom of the country is won; no marital ties till Swaraj is ours," all spoke the same word as if it were the chorus of a song.

Kandan fainted more and more, and they were helpless in the crowd. "I'm sinking—I'm sinking, Rajee, but with peace of mind, Rajee. I feel a little thirsty—will you, Rajee, will you, Sarasvati, will you, Padma, go and bring me a cup of water."

Kandan saw the sea before his very eyes and its endless lapping waters, and craved for a drop of water in his dying moment.

Rajee, Sarasvati and Padma ran to the fresh-water well on the shore and Ponnan followed them limping. But before they could return, Kandan had breathed his last. Padma stood motionless, speechless leaning on Raghu's shoulders, his bleeding right hand dressed up in a piece of cloth. Rajee held the cup of water in her hand, too late, alas!

"Alas! he died thirsting for water before it could come, alas!" Rajee said in sobbing whispers.

"Alas! he died thirsting for the freedom of his country before it could come; alas!" Sarasvati spoke to the setting sun.

"Let us remember our vow—and work out his will—that will slake, perhaps, in Heaven his thirst—our honest work on earth," Rangan said in a deep voice of resolution, like a man of deeds.

"Kandan has died a patriot-saint. Let his *samadhi* rest by the side of the tank in the very cocoanut garden where the toddy-shop once stood. Let an *ashrama* grow there for rural service, for the uplift and joy of the million poor. Kandan lives the deathless life of a patriot, a martyr," Rajee spoke, and Sarasvati nodded approval.

CHAPTER XX

THE EPILOGUE

(1)

A MONTH had passed.

It was a small room on the top flat in the *Swarajya* Office, Broadway, Madras. It was the editorial sanctum. Piles of long, lean, galley-proofs, and reams of waste printed matter, scissored and unscissored, mixed up with the live-sheets for the day were flapping in the wind, welcoming both those who came to take as well as to give. The roar of traffic outside on the road did not seem to ruffle the calm of journalistic fluency and vigour, not to mention the interruption of visitors. But the editorial pen went on spilling ink on rough paper, line after line of flaming sincerity and patriotism.

Except for a dozen pencils with shaved heads of varying degrees of longevity, there was no sign of richness in the room. Everywhere it was ink and lead; no gold, except in the firm and rich spirit of the band of young men who had all sacrificed a fine career at the bar for the service of the country at the most sacred hour of call.

The sub-editor softly opened the door which neverthless creaked on its ancient hinges, and came to the chief, looking grave, with a letter in hand. It was from a correspondent at Tranquebar. The chief read it slowly, and said in a weary voice, "Yes, feature it,—in the leading page. I'll also write a note—Rangan deserves it."

(2)

The letter appeared in bold print the same evening, and ran as follows:

Mr. A. P. Natarajan, M.A., I.C.S., the Special Magistrate in charge of the Tranquebar rioting case, delivered judgment yesterday at 6 p.m. All the accused were convicted.

R. S. Rangaswami, M.A., I.C.S., Bar-at-Law—one year R. I.

Rajeswari Bai of Bombay—six months S. I.

Sarasvati—six months S. I.

Kamakshi—six months S. I.

Ponnan—three years R. I.

Chockalinga Mudaliar—one year R. I.

Padma—one year R. I.

Raghu—one year R. I.

Nandan, Mookkan and Katteri; Irullan, Karuppan and Irullappan, and Nochi; Govindan, Pavadai, Nallan and Karian, and the other seventy-two accused, all belonging to Mr. Mudaliar's *pannai*—two years R. I. each.

Porkodi Achi, the aged mother of Chockalinga, died the same night broken-hearted on hearing the news of her only son's conviction. The great calamity that had befallen her ancient house and her only son, Chockalinga, broke her down completely in her very old age.

Ramalinga, her brother, was still there at Akkur with his daughter to comfort Porkodi in her acute distress. Though he missed for the present Chockalinga as his son-in-law, he gained the real end of his aims as he secured the management of the ancient *pannai* of Akkur.

Neelakshi, Chandru and Raghu's wife were daily present in court throughout the trial. Chandru the smart little boy of five, fearless of police shouts of 'silence' called every now and then for his *appa* and *chitappa*, Raghu and Padma, in the charming infant lisp of love that even magistracy with splendid police help could not quell.

(3)

Who could have been the special correspondent of the *Swarajya*? It was none but Sundaram, the whilom station-master of Akkur. He too was in the crowd on that fateful day. But as usual to his temperament he made himself obscure. The good luck, that was always his, did not desert him in that frightful hour. He escaped both the bullet-fire and the prosecution. The secret glands that gave him a winding, sneaking mode of approach saved him that day, and gave him back the eternal life of the truant that he so dearly loved. From the schoolboy to the wandering youth, from the wandering youth to the young *sadhu*, from the *sadhu* to the signaller, from the signaller to the station-master, from the station-master to the patriot who technically disobeyed Section 144, from the patriot to the free-lance journalist—what a career of exceeding variety to Sundaram ever since his wedding day!

(4)

In the first week of his imprisonment Padma asked himself many times in the Vellore jail:

What a hard riddle is life? What is pain, what is pleasure? What is success, what is failure? What is selfishness, what is selflessness? What is right and what is wrong? What is duty?

Young Padma, vex yourself no more with questions as ancient and difficult as the sorrows of man. Ours is the duty on earth only to do, and to do more on lines of *Dharma*. And to know in an illumined hour that all evolution is only a question of graded consciousness; how you clarify it by your own selfless thought and unattached action, and widen its range and quality. Pure *ananda* springs from such 'action' as fresh water from arid sand, the more you dig it in play, the purer and fuller it flows.

Brahmacharyam which disciplines the feed of our senses is the one known *sadhana* to attain this higher consciousness?

Instinct is life to the worm.

Reason is life to the man.

Intuition is the life of the *Gnani*.

These three grades of consciousness arise from the different levels at which each life controls and sublimates its own vital energy.

Consciousness is genius.

Genius is sublimated energy. It is *tapas*, the fruition of intense longing, striving and suffering with faith. Genius is *Brahmacharyam*. *Brahmacharyam* is a way of life, a *sadhana* that gives strength to all, to each in his own walk of life: to the romantic his wayward charm, to the public worker his strength and purity, to the poet and the musician his rhythm and deeper ecstasy, to the yogi his equipoise, and to the *Gnani*, a glimpse of the Reality and the self-realisation that makes him one with all, the crawling worm and the shining star:

THE ONE WITHOUT A SECOND

GLOSSARY

Advaitic, Monistic, (Advaita : The Sankara School of Vedanta)
Alli, Nymphaea lotus, water-lily
Ambal, Great Mother, Goddess, Consort of Siva
Ananda, Bliss
Anne, Fraternal form of address, Brother
Anni, Sister-in-law
Anthimalli, A garden-plant flowering in the evening, Mirabilis dicotoma, (nat. order, Nyctagineae)
Appa, Father
Ashrama, Hermitage, Peaceful retreat
Attar, Scent of roses
Atmagnanam, Self-realisation, Soul-science

Bairagee, Mendicant (Northern)
Bhajana, Devotional Music
Bharatavarsha, India
Brahmacharyam, a way of life that leads to self-realisation
Budmash, Rowdy

Charka, Spinning Wheel
Chitappa, Junior Paternal Uncle
Chokra, Boy

Deepavali, A Hindu Festival
Dharma, Righteousness
Dhoti, Cloth
Dorai, Boss, (European Officer, Superior)
Doraisani, European woman

Gita, The Song Celestial
Gnani, One who has attained self-realisation
Gumastha, Clerk

Iddlies, Steam-boiled rice cakes

Jagir, An Estate

Kalam, 24 Madras measures
Kaliyuga, The fourth and the worst aeon according to Hindu Mythology
Karma, The Law of Cause and Effect
Karmayogin, A man of 'action,' who does and cares not for the fruit
Karnam, Petty village officer
Karuvelam, Acacia arabica, Babul tree, (nat. order, Mimoseae)
Keertanam, Song
Khaddar, Handspun handwoven Indian cloth

Kist, Land tax
Kutti, Young girl

Lathi, Bamboo stick, one of the weapons of the Indian Police

Mahatmajiki jai, Victory to Mahatma Gandhi !
Maidan, Greensward
Maman, Uncle
Maniam, Village Officer
Mantra, Sacred incantation
Mirasdar, Landlord

Namam, caste-mark
Nanal, Reeds

Padayachi, A clan among the Sudras now devoted mainly to agriculture.

Palle, " " " "
Pan, Betel leaf
Panchami, Fifth day of the fortnight
Panchayat, indigenous Indian court
Pannai, Estate or farm
Pannaial, A serf attached to the *pannai* from generation to generation
Paracheri, The residential quarters of the pariahs
Parijatam, A beautiful flower tree, Nyctanthes arbortristis

Sadhana, The way or path to self-realisation
Sadhu, A wanderer on the Godward path
Sandhya, Sunset hour
Sannyasi, A man who has renounced the world (sadhu)
Samadhi, Tomb
Saree, Dress of the Indian ladies
Sircar, Government
Svayamvara, Free choice of husband

Tahsildar, Taluq Revenue Officer
Talayari, Village headman
Tapas, Penance

Uttappam, Rice cake

Vanni, Prosopis spicigera (nat. order, Caesalpinneae)
Veena, Stringed musical instrument
Veli, An Indian unit of land—6⅔ acres

Yejman, Master
Yoga, Process of concentration as a step to self-realisation.